W7-BC

D1010986

Praise for *Never By Chance*

"Joe Calloway, Chuck Feltz, and Kris Young have joined forces to write the book that senior management at companies large and small have been waiting for. Highly readable, loaded with innovative ideas and filled with seminal insights from both a consulting and CEO perspective, *Never By Chance* lays out a plan for aligning people and strategy to dramatically improve market share and ROI. If you're going to read one business book in 2010, this is it!"

—Kevin J. Clancy, PhD
Chairman, Copernicus Marketing Consulting

"*Never by Chance* is a real-world, pragmatic guide to authentic alignment, vision, and strategy. If you want to create enduring value for your customers that drives shareholder value, then read this book. A great read that lays out a foundational approach to aligning people, resources, and strategy."

—Kevin Cashman
Senior Partner, Korn/Ferry
Leadership & Talent Consulting Best Selling Author,
Leadership from the Inside Out

"Calloway, Feltz, and Young offer a fresh perspective on what it takes to drive business strategy to its successful conclusion. This is a compelling contribution to the literature on the application of strategy and the importance of those things that really matter. It's a must read for all those who labor in the vineyards of corporate America and those who aspire to it."

—Benjamin Ola. Akande, PhD
Dean, School of Business and Technology
Webster University

"Everyone ends up somewhere, but few end up somewhere on purpose. Doing things on purpose and for a purpose are critical to business success. *Never By Chance* makes a compelling case for intentional leadership in bringing all of a company's resources to bear on delivering the stakeholder value your organization exists to provide."

—Steve Tourek
SVP and General Counsel,
MarvinWindows and Doors

"Building and sustaining an ethical culture is key to creating value for an organization's stakeholders and real meaning in our society. *Never By Chance* provides excellent insight into the critical importance of leadership, vision and culture in aligning an organization, enhancing its business performance and fulfilling its destiny. Its practical but experienced-based approach will guide you on your journey to creating a great organization."

—Ron James
President & CEO
Center for Ethical Business Cultures
University of St. Thomas

"*Never By Chance* is exactly the message that leaders today need to not only hear, but implement. There is no more powerful catalyst for a company than a compelling vision that empowers and aligns the resources of an entire organization. *Never By Chance* is a very powerful reminder of just how important this is for any organization."

—Kevin Blair
President & CEO
NewGround

"If you want to set a clear winning direction for your business read this book. Learn the power of an impactful vision that inspires your people to excel. Build a culture of ethics and respect that motivates your team to passionate customer focus. *Never By Chance* provides clear and simple direction that will help propel your long term business success."

—Joe Scarlett
Founder, The Scarlett Leadership Institute

NEVER
BY

Aligning People and
Strategy Through
Intentional Leadership

CHANCE

JOE CALLOWAY   CHUCK FELTZ   KRIS YOUNG

WILEY

John Wiley & Sons, Inc.

To Annette, Jessica, and Cate. You are my constant joy.
—Joe Calloway

*To Janelle, Audrey and Andrea, the most important people
in my life. Thank you for your support and confidence.*
—Chuck Feltz

*For my two very grown-up kids, Jenny and John, whom
I love with a passion.*
—Kris Young

CONTENTS

INTRODUCTION

WHITE HOT

Ask any business leader how tough today's environment is and they'll most likely tell you they've never worked harder. Many talk of an environment where the pressure to deliver has reached a "white hot" level of intensity, where careers that used to be measured in decades are now measured in a couple of years (or months!), and where product and company lifecycles move from inception to commodity status in record time.

They will also tell you that, in spite of cost management taking center stage, many of them have more initiatives to handle now than ever before: Enterprise solutions, new go-to-market strategies, acquisition planning, expedited product development, new manufacturing strategies, downsizing, internal start ups, online strategies, employee engagement programs, supply chain management, technology upgrades, talent development, succession planning, disruptive competitors, and governance standard development are just some of the concerns that currently drive daily activity in countless organizations. The "more with less" mantra has never been more prevalent; and it is imperative that leaders deliver greater results with fewer resources in less time. "Daunting" would not be an overstatement in describing the challenge.

We recently heard from one particular leader that, despite everything her company was doing, she was still very frustrated with the pace of progress in delivering their business strategy. Although they were running at full speed and had a packed slate of initiatives, it still didn't feel as though they were "hitting on all cylinders" or were as aligned as they could be. The sense that they were "leaving too much on the table" not only made for some sleepless nights; it triggered some very real consequences in how the business operated. As sustainable results were slower in coming, the firm was quick to question the core strategy. This incited what this executive called the "annual strategy rework," with a new strategy being layered on top of the old one year after year—before the organization had even begun to absorb the previous one. Over time, this approach conditioned employees to expect the next "silver bullet" or, even worse, to adopt a "this, too, shall pass" mentality regarding the strategy—something that inhibits employee engagement when it is needed the most.

It was with this challenging environment in mind that we decided to write *Never By Chance*.

OUR POINT OF VIEW

We knew from our first discussion about this book that we wanted to leverage each of our unique backgrounds to provide a well-rounded and thoughtful perspective on what we believed was a key issue facing leaders today.

Chuck Feltz has been a successful C-level leader of both public and private companies in multiple industries that range in size and scope—from an international startup to a Fortune 500 company. He is widely recognized for his innovative business strategies and visionary leadership that drive shareholder value in the companies he has led. His "feet on the ground" operating style and leadership experience were perspectives we felt the reader would value.

Joe Calloway has been a popular business advisor for almost 30 years. He has helped literally hundreds of companies and thousands of people create and sustain success. Joe has studied success factors across a wide range of businesses and has spoken on performance issues at thousands of events. Joe is the author of three other books: *Indispensable—How to Become the Company That Your Customers Can't Live Without; Work Like You're Showing Off!;* and the best-selling *Becoming a Category of One: How Extraordinary Companies Transcend Commodity and Defy Comparison.*

For over 17 years, Kris Young has designed experiences that engage employees and customers with companies' visions. She is an expert in creating events that compel strategic execution and has worked with the top global business speakers on a wide variety of corporate meetings. In 2007, Kris was named the National Speakers Association Meeting Partner of the Year.

Our goal in writing the book was very simple: We wanted to help companies and their leaders answer the question, "How do we increase the effectiveness and speed of our business strategy?" We wanted them to be confident in their ability to do more with less—not paralyzed by it. And finally, we wanted leaders to rest easier knowing that every resource they had was laser focused on making their vision a reality.

AN INTENTIONAL MINDSET

When we consider how resources are used, we typically think of the effort and thought that goes into traditional asset deployment (plants, real estate, equipment) in order to create return for shareholders. What's less certain is how consciously the resources that are not on the balance sheet are utilized to create value. These powerful elements are too often left to chance in terms of how strategically they are managed—for several reasons:

- They are considered to be "soft" or intangible assets that do not drive quantifiable return.
- They aren't owned by anyone in particular in the organization.
- Most leaders do not have a process in place to derive value from these.

In times when resources are constrained (and they almost always are) and leaders are still held to incredibly high standards for creating value, it is a mistake to leave the strategic leverage of these resources to chance.

In companies that do this well, it is less about a tactical approach and more about a mindset. Leaders who deliver successfully in all types of conditions and economies approach the situation aggressively by saying: "Any resource that *can* be valuable *will* be valuable." Whether it is tangible or intangible is irrelevant. They apply the same intentional approach to aligning and managing these resources as they do to the "hard assets" and consider this one of their primary obligations because they know that, with the right level of intention, effort, and creativity, these intangible resources create real value. They realize these resources already exist within their organizations and are not incremental additions that drive more cost. The benefit comes from their intentional development and utilization and is grounded in the belief that if these resources already exist, it is simply smart business to put them to work more effectively on behalf of your stakeholders.

But, more than anything, company leaders know that, when these *existing* resources are treated in this manner, they can have a hugely disproportionate benefit. Not only do they create value in and of themselves; but they also act as catalysts that enhance other assets and accelerate the strategy's overall delivery. For this reason, this mindset cannot be an elective for leaders looking to deliver maximum value on behalf of employees, clients, and shareholders.

RETURN ON EVERY RESOURCE

It's important that leaders can clearly answer the question, "Am I getting the most return on every resource at my disposal on behalf of stakeholders?" However, it's not a one-time question. Companies must be able to constantly self-diagnose their situations to recognize the "alerts" that signal the need for a new approach or operating perspective. Consider the following list of indicators as a good starting point:

1. You're frustrated with the pace of your progress, even though you have "all hands on deck" and couldn't imagine being any busier.

2. Your customer experience is inconsistently executed, or you have no intentional design being delivered across all of your customer touch points.

3. You rarely share your vision openly and aggressively with employees and other key stakeholders as the context for "why you are doing what you are doing."

4. You don't feel your teams "get" the strategy like you do; you're one of few people in your company who can clearly describe how all the pieces come together and make sense; employees complain that initiatives seem isolated and one hand doesn't know what the other is doing.

5. Operations simply seem too complicated; your teams are constantly asking, "Does it really have to be this hard?"

6. You seem to spend more time planning strategy than executing it; strategies change too frequently and old ones are layered on top of new ones.

7. Your employees are not as engaged as you think they should be, given the significance of the challenges and opportunities you are facing.

8. Your executive team cannot clearly describe how your culture is a competitive advantage in your marketplace *from the customers' perspective.*

9. Your sales teams are getting less contact with higher level decision makers than they used to; they complain that customers just want cheaper prices. There's more concern than there used to be about your product or service becoming a commodity.

ABOUT THE CHAPTERS

Though this book is about aligning people and strategy, you won't see separate chapters on either "people" or "strategy." While each organization's strategy will be different, there are several key similarities: Each wants theirs to be as effective and successful as it can be and accomplished in the shortest time possible. For that reason, we analyzed the key factors that exist in every organization that can make this happen—and how we can intentionally align them for maximum results.

Accordingly, each chapter is dedicated to one of the foundational factors critical to executing your strategy most effectively. Each chapter was written with the mindset that, if you were going to invest the time to read it, it should contain information that could immediately be used to drive your strategy faster—and without adding significant cost. Each chapter also identifies and defines each undervalued resource and how to determine whether you are getting its maximum value. We also provide short case studies of companies who have excelled at these strategies because we feel that it's important to see what this looks like in action when it's done well in the "real world."

We begin with the chapter on Vision, the genesis of strategy and one of the most powerful (and underutilized) resources at our disposal. A deliberately designed vision is a powerful tool for establishing a working context for making decisions and encouraging behavior in a company. It provides the ambition that propels an organization forward, sustains it through difficult times, and answers the question, "What will we look like when we succeed?" We will discuss how important it is to create a compelling vision with all stakeholders in mind and not simply tactically generating one for a specific event (analysts call, annual report, board meeting, etc.).

"Culture As a Competitive Advantage" discusses how you can consciously *design and showcase* your firm's culture in a way that distinguishes you from your competitors and drives maximum employee engagement. We want to answer the question, "What should we stand for in our organization that helps make our vision a reality?"

The chapter on Relevance encourages you to look at your organization objectively and ask, "Do our customers think we are as important to them as we do?" Market changes, technology, new competitors, and even an organization's historical success create blindspots that can cause its level of customer relevance to slip away. How you handle the things that matter most to your clients and customers is critical to maintaining your standing with them. We'll teach you how to audit your relevance and increase your position on your customers' "Relevance Hierarchy."

We then delve into the role Customer Experience plays as an accelerator of your business strategy. There's never a case where you do *not* have a customer experience; it's just a matter of whether it is intended to enhance your business strategy or just a collection of random behaviors occurring at your customer touch points. The first promotes value, employee engagement, and pride, while the second advances a fractured strategy that leaves customers at best underwhelmed and at worst broadcasters to the world of how little they think of your company.

In our Special Report on Events As Strategy, we'll discuss this underleveraged asset and challenge the tendency to schedule our next event or meeting simply because "we do it this time every year". Company meeting and event strategy management is a vital asset in the execution of your overall business strategy. It is a powerful tool for leaders to engage and focus employees on the vision and the key role each of them play in making this a reality.

Finally, the chapter on Intentional Leadership supports our foundational perspective that an organization's leaders are uniquely positioned—even *obligated*—to purposefully develop and execute this level of strategic alignment. Due to their complex and cross-functional nature, these responsibilities simply cannot be initiated and executed at a grass roots level. When left unattended by the leaders, organizations will deliver sub-optimal performance. However, when leaders fulfill this obligation and execute accordingly, they have the power to start a wave of cascading success that will benefit customers, employees, and shareholders alike. Their message will be loud and clear: that their leadership and success will always be intentional and *Never By Chance*.

FINAL THOUGHTS

A Google search of the term "leadership books" delivers 36.6 million hits. Clearly, we didn't decide to write *Never By Chance* because there was a shortage of material on the subject of leadership. We wrote this book because we have experienced, witnessed, and in some cases *caused* the level of frustration that comes from running an organization at breakneck speed with so much in play that you can barely keep track of it. We know that many organizations take seductive comfort in thinking, "We couldn't be any busier or jam any more into our days; therefore we must be making progress"—only to later realize that *how much* is going on means much less than *how* it is going on.

Given the incredible demands to grow value—and the very short windows of time in which to do so—companies have decidedly short attention spans and think nothing of layering one strategy on top of another, confusing employees, customers and shareholders alike. Again, if the definition of success is the constant churn of direction, activity, and resources, then this is perfect. But, at some point, measurable and sustainable success is essential. We can take no comfort in activity without results.

All but a very few organizations are forced to deal with significant resource constraints. The intelligent and judicious use of assets is critical for creating new value and growth; none can be overlooked or squandered. Purposefully aligning and delivering more value from existing assets and resources ("more with less") has become the coveted "magic potion." The bad news is, as always, that there is no magic. The *good* news is that there *is* a way to draw out the value in *existing* resources that lie dormant in many organizations. It is this intentional alignment of resources and people with strategy that has the power to catalyze an organization.

We wish you success.

1

VISION

Begin With the End in Mind

There is nothing more powerful than an organization whose resources are laser-focused on a vision that every employee clearly understands—so much so that they wake up each morning knowing their role in making that vision a reality.

A COMPELLING VIEW OF THE FUTURE

Chuck: Pick up any annual report; find the chairman's message to shareholders and read the vision statement—the description of what the company aspires to be, what they will achieve, and how they will accomplish this.

Now go to any employee in the company (maybe your company) and ask him or her to tell you the company's vision. Compare that response to the annual report message. Now ask another employee and maybe even a couple more. How consistent are the replies? In much of our work, we find the responses to be surprisingly consistent. They sound something like this, "Our vision? Well, we make (fill in the blank with the product)." Then read the vision statement to these employees and ask them how it affects what they do every day; in other words, how do they act differently knowing what the vision is? The difference between what we *make* and what we strive to *become* are worlds apart.

Is it the lack of a vision that is the issue? Not really. Most companies have a vision somewhere that they put together for an annual report, a shareholder meeting, or as the result of an offsite planning retreat.

But the mere existence of a vision statement is not the goal. There are more than enough visions out there, full of jargon and "corporate speak" that only those who created them could really begin to understand.

What we are talking about is something far beyond the obligatory sanitized versions of "vision statements" that appear in many annual reports or corporate brochures. Rather, we mean a view of the future so compelling that it causes employees to get up every morning aspiring to achieve it—not only because they believe in it, but because they *clearly understand* their personal roles in accomplishing it. Likewise, your vision can distinguish your value proposition in the eyes of your customers and enhance their desire to align with your company. A vision at this level becomes the cornerstone and the context that steers all organizational choices and actions. It answers the most important question your employees will ever ask you: "Why are we doing what we are doing?"

WHAT'S THE DEAL?

Joe: I often like to surpass the specific concept of vision and instead ask more general questions of people in an organization. If I were to ask your employees, "What's the deal with you guys? What are you all about? What's the point of all this that you're doing?" What would their answers be? Think about all of your employees—certainly not just management or the leadership team. How would the receptionist, somebody from the IT department, or one of the guys or gals in the warehouse answer the question, "What's the deal with you guys?"

Sadly, members of most organizations wouldn't quite understand the question. The response would most likely be some form of, "I don't get it. What do you mean 'what's the deal with us?'" As Chuck said, if they had any answer at all, they'd probably respond with "we make computers" or "we do industrial cleaning" or "we are accountants." All of these are fine things to make, do, and be; but it's not the point. And it's not smart business.

What answer do I frequently get from members of companies that have people and strategy aligned? What do employees in companies with intentional leadership that has embraced the responsibility of driving a clear vision throughout the organization say about purpose? If I ask, "What's the deal with you guys?" there will be no hesitation. They'll tell me exactly what the deal is with them; and they'll go on to articulate the firm's vision, not as a memorized slogan, but in their own words and with their own grasp of what they aspire to be, what they want to achieve, and exactly how they will accomplish it. And most important—they will tell you exactly what role they play in all of this.

ALIGNING EVERY RESOURCE

Chuck: It would be easy to characterize this work simply as "just doing the right thing" and making certain people "feel good" about what they do (which, by the way, isn't a bad thing). But it goes well beyond that. Leaders of organizations want to create a compelling vision for one reason: to deliver the greatest value for customers and, as a result, employees and shareholders. And our best opportunity to do that is by putting *every* resource we have toward that end. No wasted effort, no isolated projects that don't support the vision, no meaningless (and endless) meetings, and certainly no disengaged or apathetic employees uncertain of how what they do matters in the greater scheme of things.

An intentionally crafted vision will engage, enlighten, and give greater purpose to our employees' work, which is a noble outcome in and of itself. In the end, however, leaders are obligated to develop value on behalf of all of our stakeholders. By failing to leverage the power of a strong and purposeful vision, we never realize the return of one of our most powerful assets and we default on one of our key responsibilities as leaders. Strength and clarity of vision are the key catalysts of employee empowerment and engagement and the foundation for aligning an organization's strategy and resources.

A LIFE LESSON IN THE VALUE OF VISION

Chuck: Prior to starting my business career, I worked in a private hospital on a Physical Rehabilitation team counseling patients who had suffered significant trauma and their families. I remember one patient in particular who taught me one of the most valuable lessons I have ever learned about the power of a compelling vision (sometimes we learn our best lessons outside of our business environments).

Janet was a young mother admitted to the hospital after a horrendous car accident that left her paralyzed from the mid-chest down. Her rehabilitation was going to be measured in years, not months; and her days were made up of three excruciating therapy rituals where a good day meant walking down the parallel bars 10 feet unassisted. A bad day—and they were countless—would end in frustration, tears, and anger, only to get up the next day to do it all over again. On top of all this, Janet was facing a prognosis that would have depressed even the most optimistic of us. Yet we marveled at her tenacity and conviction in the face of this unthinkable tragedy.

Janet and I spoke often about her challenges and her preparation to go home. I still remember one of those conversations like it was yesterday. It had been a grueling morning for her that ended with her collapsing face down on the floor, bloodying her nose and spraining her arm. While we waited for her physician, we discussed her frustration with the temporary setback. I mentioned to her that she had become quite an inspiration to her rehab team because of the relentless dedication she showed in her therapy. I told her that we were in awe of her ability to maintain this level of incredible effort day in and day out.

With blood still running from her nose and holding her injured arm at her side, Janet quietly pulled a picture of her two daughters from the pocket of her hospital gown. "Before we had the girls, Steve (her husband) and I talked about the type of parents we envisioned ourselves to be. We promised one another we would be the best mother and father we could imagine and knew *exactly* what that meant to each of us. I have no intention of wavering on that; it is my personal vision. This is who I want to be. The only difference is that now I will be doing this from a wheelchair."

Janet was able to cross one of the deepest chasms imaginable because of the power of the vision she had for herself. She refused to allow her accident to alter who she intended to be and every resource she could muster was aligned to realize this. Something that would have made many of us completely redefine our lives and what we stood for was for her an interruption on the path toward a clear and focused outcome.

Never underestimate the power of a clear and compelling vision, in life or in business.

VISION-DRIVEN BEHAVIOR

Joe: From the power to change a life right down to the power of deciding what you should do in the next hour, a clear, compelling vision can bring powerful intention and alignment. That's why a vision should never be anything less than a living, breathing guide to every decision that's made in an organization—no matter how small that decision may seem.

I was speaking to an audience of about 80 people in a downtown Toronto hotel ballroom during a leadership meeting for a financial services client. In the middle of my presentation, the service door behind me opened and in walked a hotel employee with a tray of full water pitchers. Without a word—or any acknowledgment that there were people in the room or a presentation taking place—he began to replace the empty water pitchers on the tables with full ones. He banged and clanged his way through the room, walking in front of people—including myself—as he purposefully carried out his task. He was focused and doing a good job of replacing empty water pitchers. Unfortunately, the job he was doing was in direct conflict with part of the hotel's stated vision: to create an environment conducive to productivity and effective meetings.

The waiter was so fixed on his task that he missed the overall point, which, of course, was for us to have a productive meeting. Though his momentary task was to replace empty water pitchers with full ones, it was a shame that he didn't let the company vision drive his behavior. Disrupting the meeting and distracting everyone in the room created the exact opposite effect of what the hotel staff should consider most important.

Vision should drive everything. What is the desired overall outcome? How can I best serve my customer, coworker, vendor, or community in the interest of fulfilling it? Sometimes even with the best of intentions we sacrifice the big picture by having counterproductive tunnel vision. This hotel employee, for instance, would have served the group's interests much better by waiting until a scheduled break to replace the water pitchers.

A balance takes place here, where to be fully engaged means to be totally present and intentional about the task at hand—yet also understanding how to make the greatest contribution toward achieving the vision.

This is the stuff that cartoons and clichés are made of: the short-sighted company policy that handcuffs employees in the interest of maintaining control over expenses—at the very expense of customer satisfaction, which ultimately determines the organization's fate. Short-term concerns over not "giving away the store" become the very reason that the store goes out of business—the vision to build a business based on lasting relationships was either ignored or never understood in the first place.

CONNECTED TO REALITY

It's truly amazing how often I see companies whose behavior does not connect in any way to the stated vision. I sometimes shop at a neighborhood grocery store that is part of a regional chain. This store advertises that they have "good value—low prices—and great taste." I can't argue with the fact that they deliver pretty well on all three of those promises. But there's a disconnect.

Standing in the checkout line one day, I noticed the company's vision statement posted on a big sign on the store's front wall. It said, in part, that their goal was "to be the very best, most progressive, and innovative neighborhood store in America." Okay, well, let's think for a minute. This grocery store is a couple of blocks from a Trader Joe's grocery store and about three blocks from a Whole Foods grocery store, both of which are very progressive and innovative stores. It's also right across the street from an Apple Store, which may well be *the single most* progressive and innovative store in America.

Now don't get me wrong; I shop at this grocery store because I like it. They do a good job. But the thing that stands out about them especially is selection. They've got everything you could possibly want and carry every major brand that's out there. *That's* where they have an edge on the likes of Trader Joe's and Whole Foods—not in innovation! You certainly don't want to claim that you are attempting to be the most progressive and innovative store around when you're right across the street from an Apple Store unless you are truly engaging in some knock-your-socks-off innovation.

I actually don't see anything particularly progressive or innovative in this store at all. Why in the world would they have that as their vision—and then completely ignore it? Either they are doing the wrong things or they've got the wrong vision. Frankly, I think it's the latter. They should retool their vision statement so to steer the behavior they want (and are already quite good at); and *that* will enable them to differentiate, create value, and ultimately succeed.

An effective vision has to connect directly with the reality of the company's everyday events. Otherwise, it's not only pointless; it may in fact confuse everyone from employees to customers.

MATTERING

Chuck: After years of leading organizations, I've noticed that most people very much want to be a part of something bigger than themselves—to know that what they do 40, 50, or 60 hours a week actually makes a difference.

I believe this holds true for even the most cynical among us. Rare is the person who, when asked, "What do you do for a living?" is comfortable responding, "Well, nothing really. I just go in every day and do what they tell me to do. No one really notices or cares and then I just go back and do it again the next day."

This is in no way meant to suggest that a person's self-worth and reason for existing should depend solely upon their work. However, it does mean that, since people spend up to one half of their waking hours doing a particular job, they want to know that its significance carries beyond the activity itself. Being able to "see yourself" in the bigger picture and knowing the purpose of what you do is one of the most important ways to engage employees. Creating a powerful and compelling vision that lets others see that what they do every hour of every day truly matters in the greater scheme of things is incredibly important. Why? Because it addresses one of our basic human needs: to know we have a purpose in something greater than ourselves.

Now, if that causes some of us to think, "Okay fine, *whatever*, then it's the employees' responsibility to figure it out for themselves," then we need to pause for a moment and ask: "In the end, who has the ultimate responsibility to deliver greater value in the company by aligning existing resources in the most effective manner?"

A quick look in the mirror answers our question. As leaders, we're *uniquely* positioned to align vision, strategy, and people. It is one of the highest return and lowest cost strategies we can deploy—and, one of the fundamental obligations of leadership. Left to chance it will not happen on its own. But an intentional, focused leader can cause this to happen in an organization and as a result, drive greater success for everyone.

I GET IT . . . WHY DOESN'T EVERYONE ELSE?

Joe: It's not enough that, as the leader of an organization, you totally "get it" in terms of understanding the vision. Everyone else has to get it, too; your most fundamental job requirement is to make sure that happens. You can't print the vision on a wallet card or put it in the power point presentation and think that, since all of your employees can read, they will embrace and live according to it. There's a distinction between logically "understanding" the vision and emotionally "getting" it. If the members of your organization don't comprehend the latter, you will find it extremely difficult to sustain success. If you've got a company full of people who have made *only* a logical, intellectual commitment, then you are at serious risk of failing. That might sound like a bold assertion, but it's one that I completely stand by.

If, however, your employees are intellectually *and emotionally* committed, then you are in a much better position. You have to have both of these; and a vision that turns you on had better turn your people on, too. A commitment to a job is pretty weak stuff to try and grow a business with. Commitment to "this is what I do with my life because it is truly important to me" is infinitely stronger.

THE EMPLOYEE CHOICE

Chuck: When we ask an employee to "get on board" and fully connect with an organization, we sometimes forget that the employee requires a lot of information to consciously make this very important choice. Of course, many simply respond with the politically correct response and say they are "ready to go." But I'm not talking about that type of buy in; I'm talking about a heart and mind commitment—the kind that reminds you *why* you are committed, *what* you are focused on, and that makes you feel as if you can't get to work fast enough each day. That kind of commitment can only come from having the right knowledge and information. And that must come from one place-you as the leader.

To facilitate such a commitment, an organization's leadership must first offer the right information to employees. This includes a vivid description on where the company is going, how they will get there, and why they will succeed. The most effective way to accomplish this is to so tightly align vision and strategy that every employee understands what the organization is doing, what success looks like, and their role in accomplishing it.

This level of information sharing is critical in order for the leaders to drive the inflection point I call the "Employee Choice"—the moment when they can say to their employee teams, "I have fulfilled my obligation to tell you where our company is headed, how we will succeed, and the role we will ask you to play to help us get there. We can't get there without you. I now want you to use this information so that you can make the important choice to go with us."

Leaders who do this well achieve one of three possible (and intended) outcomes:

- First, their employees get it, see it, and are ready to go. Everything makes sense, and they willingly engage. If you have done your work well, a very large percentage of your employees will react in this way.

- Second, they want to go forward with you, but they have questions and need legitimate clarification on what you have told them to help them make this commitment. In these cases, we must commit ourselves to helping any team members work through this and to making certain that we have clearly communicated what they need in order for them to make this important decision. This will be the second-largest group of employees.

- Third, they find that (for whatever reason—perhaps a lack of confidence in the direction, strategy, or leadership) they do not want to "sign up." It is vitally important that company leaders recognize this choice as a legitimate one, to be honored accordingly. Well-informed employees who "self-select" out after having the best information on which to base their decisions have made a respectable choice; and their move to another area, division or company should be handled with the utmost respect and dignity. There is no vision or strategy 100 percent of people will agree with. While this third faction will be the smallest group of employees, it is an important one because the organization will be watching to see how they are handled. Dignity and respect are the keywords here.

For the benefit of the organization, there is a fourth choice that must be avoided. It is when an employee who understands the company's direction and their role in it, chooses not to engage or leave. Instead, they simply stay, put their time in, keep their head down, and avoid responsibilities that other team members will have to bear. Today's companies are too lean and employee teams too interdependent to allow this. Not only is it unfair and disrespectful to those who made the choice to stay and fully engage, it compromises the value the company needs to deliver to customers and shareholders.

The only way to responsibly eliminate this undesirable fourth choice and push for this level of commitment is for leaders to empower their employees with clarity about the organization's course and resulting expectations. If this component is missing, the "employee choice" cannot be made in earnest. It is instead based on supposition and opinion rather than fact—neither of which creates a good outcome for such a critical choice.

The power of an intentionally developed and well-communicated vision that informs employees of a company's aspirations, intended accomplishments, and how they will achieve them is one of the most underutilized assets in business today. When done well, it is an engaging position that creates competitive distinction for a company and engages its employee teams by establishing a context for their action and behavior.

I've been asked whether this "choice" and "conversation" happens literally or figuratively. My answer is both, depending on the condition of the business and the urgency of the change needed. I've had these discussions with individuals and with teams of several thousand employees at one time; and I have been informed on more than one occasion that this could be risky. Perhaps, but not nearly as risky as leaving the opportunity to truly engage tens, hundreds, or thousands of employees to chance. That's a risk leaders simply cannot take.

A GOOD JOB VERSUS THE RIGHT JOB

Joe: The old joke that says, "We don't know where we're going, but we're making good time" isn't very funny when it comes to your business. Too many leaders focus on "strategy execution" when instead what they need to do is step back and determine whether the strategy even makes sense in the first place. Your people may be doing a good job, but are they doing the *right* job? It's the old "efficiency versus effectiveness" question. So how do you know whether the appropriate tasks are getting accomplished? That's why you have a vision.

For example: If your goal is to be the lowest-cost airline and you're focusing on how to serve the best in-flight meals in the industry, then of course you're going to be out of whack. People in your company are working night and day to cut costs, while others are spending all their time trying to find the tastiest salad dressing. Your initial vision has pretty much already determined that you shouldn't serve in-flight meals at all. You're there to be the lowest-cost airline, not the best treat airline. Pick a lane and stay there. That's what your vision does for you.

MEASURING AND REWARDING THE WRONG THING

Intentional leadership aligns people with strategy. Consider what you measure and reward, and whether or not your strategy achieves this end. Many companies measure and reward behavior on a daily basis that is absolutely counterproductive to the realization of the vision. Again, people are doing their tasks well, but they're completing the wrong tasks.

A client of mine did some remarkable work with a group of banks who joined together to study the challenge and opportunity of customer problem resolution. They focused on their call center operations, where most customers voice their complaints and problems. The bankers in the study said that they had expected their work to be about developing better scripts for the call center employees to use when resolving problems. What they ultimately discovered, however, was aligning people with strategy would create the most opportunity in this arena.

Surprisingly, most companies measure the length of the call in their call centers. They operate under the assumption that the faster you can turn the calls, the less time customers will have to wait, and the happier everyone will be. Efficiency will win the day. But when you look at a strategy of minimizing length of calls through the lens of the banks' vision statements, there is a serious disconnect.

Every one of the banks in the study said that creating high-quality relationships with customers was a priority. Some of them even had wording to that effect right in the vision statement. So think about it. Their stated priority is high-quality relationships; yet they measure and reward their employees based on getting those pesky customers off the phone as quickly as possible. What? If the goal is to create significant connections with customers, then shouldn't they throw the scripts away and turn off all the clocks? Yes, they should. That's called alignment. You let your people be human beings with customers instead of script-readers. You take your time and ensure that the problems are resolved in a way that maximizes the customers' satisfaction and appreciation. You do what *you said you were going to do* in the vision. You make important through measurement and reward what you originally claimed was so vital in the vision.

GET IN FRONT OF EVERYONE

Chuck: About a year ago, I was working with a financial services CEO and his four-person team. We met in an off-site location where we spent two full days together to review and create a new retail banking experience for them. As part of the session, we had asked the CEO to present an overview of their strategic plan to my partners, so that we could fully comprehend the vision and business strategy of the organization.

The CEO gave a 30-minute presentation to open our work together. He very appropriately started with the vision, which he used with Wall Street analysts. He then moved on to outline the business strategy and described how it would make the vision a reality on behalf of shareholders and employees. He was passionate, articulate and laid a strong foundation for our work together.

Later that evening, one of his team members came up to me after dinner and said she wanted to thank me for setting up this meeting. I told her we were pleased to do it and looked forward to a very productive couple of days together, given how well the first one had gone. She agreed, and said, "Not only that, it was great to hear David (the CEO) talk about his vision. We never hear him talk about our future like that when we are back at the office; and we have been dying to know how he's been thinking about our future. Now everything we are doing makes so much more sense—and it's very exciting. I'm going to ask him if I can pass this on to my team when we get home."

In retrospect, I hope the look on my face didn't give away my thoughts; however, I'm fairly certain it did. We had just spent a 10-hour day with the top team at a leading financial institution, and one of the biggest perks for this EVP (the number 3 person) was that she got to hear the CEO talk about their vision and where the organization was heading. She even wanted to know if it *would be okay* to share it with her employees! I had to wonder how she, as a top officer of this company, would have ever learned about her own organization's vision had we not initiated this session.

The key takeaway: A secret vision is a worthless vision. To assume that only the top team or person needs to get it is unacceptable—and tantamount to leaving one of the most powerful tools that a leader has on the table. If you have a strong and compelling vision you are proud to talk about, get in front of everyone with it. And if you don't, then create one you do believe in.

GET ON BOARD WITH *WHAT*?

Joe: Many years ago, I was participating in a planning session for a company's annual employee meeting. The CEO had come in to give us his vision for the event. For 15 minutes, he told us that leadership had to get on board and get every employee on board with them. He pointed out that they had good people and good products, but that they needed everyone to work together. By the end of his talk, everyone in the room was pretty clear that his goal for this upcoming meeting was to "get everyone on board."

After the CEO left the room, we all just looked at each other. There was an uncomfortable silence—much like what you may have experienced when having dinner at your great aunt's house and there is only the sound of rustling napkins because no one knows what to say. In this case, however, the discomfort was caused by the fact that everyone knew what to say; and finally, one brave soul did: "Get on board with *what*?"

This was a company that didn't know who it was. If you had asked 50 of its employees what they were all about and what the point of it all was, you would have heard a variety of answers, the most common being, "I don't have the first clue." Anyone could tell you what they were selling; but no one could tell you where they were going. The CEO seemed to think that, if everyone just "got on board" with whatever was in front of them, everything would be fine. Performance would win out.

But excelling at tasks that have no point, no alignment with what everyone else is doing, and no emotional payoff for the employee is an exercise in setting speed records in a hamster's wheel. There are countless companies that do a good job at things that don't matter—neither to employees, nor to the marketplace. Ultimately, those companies go out of business.

RELENTLESS TALK

Chuck: The notion of "getting in front of everyone" means exactly that. Companies who deliver added value through the leverage of their vision relentlessly talk about it to their employees and—interestingly enough—to their shareholders, private investors, clients, suppliers, and anyone else who will listen. Why? Because they have intentionally designed their vision to be used in front of multiple audiences. This can be a tremendous source of pride and engagement for employee teams. Nothing instills more confidence in leadership than knowing that their leaders clearly "get it" and are willing to include them in "being in the know" with them. Additionally, it will give investors confidence that this company knows where it intends to go and will effectively align their resources in a manner that will create significant and measurable returns for them. And in front of a client or customer, this can be a powerful point of competitive distinction. We used to make certain ours was in front of our competition (not hard in a public company) because we wanted them to know exactly what they were up against; and *we* wanted to define the rules of the game, instead of leaving it up to them.

THE LANGUAGE OF VISION

Joe: Many companies have vision statements written in flawless corporate-speak, often devoid of emotion, and therefore meaningless. It may be printed on pocket cards that every employee is required to carry or read aloud at the annual meeting. And few, if any, employees have any personal connection to it or feeling about it at all.

If your vision statement doesn't strike an emotional chord in employees, then what is its point? We're talking about a *vision*, not procedural guidelines. It should be something that any and every employee can verbalize succinctly and in their own words—not as some memorized slogan.

At a managers' meeting for a chain of emergency medical care clinics, I pressed one of the participants to tell me—in her own words—what the point of the company was. After a great deal of resistance (for fear of giving a "wrong" answer), she finally said, "Hey, we help people when they're hurt! Okay?"

Yes. Okay, indeed. I asked the group if any of them were particularly inspired by the company's vision statement. Not a single one said yes. I then asked if they were inspired by this woman's six-word vision statement: "We help people when they're hurt." Every hand in the room was raised.

State your vision simply, powerfully, and with emotion. Rev. Martin Luther King, Jr. didn't inspire anyone by saying, "I have a strategic plan with the following bulleted points." He said, "I have a dream." Your mission should tap into employees' hearts and dreams. If it doesn't, then what's the point?

EMPLOYEES OUT OF ALIGNMENT

Chuck: Communication of the vision throughout the organization should be one of the most significant and rewarding interaction opportunities we have with our employees. Yet companies too often fail to capitalize on this opportunity. Rather than a personal, engaging interaction, in far too many cases, it looks more like a talking head video that is given to department leaders, who then call their teams together and say, "Here is a video of Steve, our CEO, talking about our vision."

Afterwards, the five-minute video is over and the manager asks, "Any questions?" Assuming there are any, rarely is the manager equipped to answer with any level of meaningful content or to engage in a strategic conversation to help the employees really internalize what they have heard. In one client department meeting we attended, a line worker asked, "Can you tell us what he meant when he talked about how our strategy has changed?" To which the department manager said, "You just saw the video, so you know as much as I know," and he then went on to cover the department's other agenda topics.

His response wouldn't have been described as the height of engagement or communication effectiveness; and you can bet it wasn't what the CEO meant when he said, "Let's get this message out." It's not at all hard to see why leaders get so frustrated when they think they have done the important work of passing down the knowledge to the entire organization—only to find that it's barely made it out of their offices.

But who's at fault here? The department manager who was told to show the talking head video? The employee who is trying to get it but can't receive the answers she needs to understand it? Or the leadership who assumed that hundreds of hours of context development and incredibly important work could be delivered in a well-meaning but completely ineffective manner? This often used approach has the unintended consequence of actually diminishing the value of the time spent in crafting the strategy and vision in the first place.

To leave hundreds or thousands of employees out of alignment compromises the value we are tasked to create. Employees need to learn by asking, engaging, and internalizing in their own way. This doesn't mean personal counseling sessions with every employee; it just means recognizing how your employees learn and structuring the communication of your strategy and vision accordingly. It means getting top leaders face to face with employees to communicate, explain and "honor the debate" as each employee seeks to understand in their own personal way.

Only then can you expect them to buy in on what you have spent hundreds of collective hours designing.

I OWE HIM THAT

The ownership of the vision must come from the top before it can be shared across an organization. This is the principal role of leadership: defining where we will go, why, and how we will win. It cannot be discussed enough because it is the context for maintaining everything that comes after. Top leadership must be certain that every leader in the organization can articulate the vision in his or her authentic voice and be held accountable to do that. This is critical.

Is it hard work? Very. There will be times when you will be tired of hearing yourself talk, when you feel you simply can't talk about it anymore. In an interview with Lou Gehrig, one of the greatest baseball players of all time, a reporter asked, "Lou, after the thousands of games you have played, there must be days when you come to the park and just don't feel that you can give 100 percent, that you just go through the motions. It happens even to the best doesn't it?" To which Lou responded, "Actually, no it doesn't. When I come to the park and see that 10-year-old child watching me from the stands, I know this is likely the first time he has ever seen Lou Gehrig play; and I play for him like I played when it was my first time on the field. I owe him that." As leaders, we owe our teams the same level of passion and conviction in communicating the future success of our organizations.

NOTHING LEFT TO CHANCE

Chuck: So ask yourself: If the leadership doesn't do this—then who does? Isn't that what we're obligated to do? Designing a compelling view of the future is only as effective as the passionate and intentional way it is communicated to those whose lives it will affect. Deliver your message as if it is going to change the course of your organization forever—because it can. Don't simply throw something together to get it off of your to do list.

Companies that do communicate well-designed visions can have a great effect on redefining the purpose of certain functional areas. As an example: A company that realized that its new vision required an entirely new skill set in its customer-facing areas decided to retrain and repopulate all of their call centers. It became clear that the entire recruiting, assessment, and on-boarding process had to change.

As HR internalized the new plan, they appropriately asked the question, "Given this direction, how should we behave to ensure the success of our vision?" It quickly became clear that they found themselves in the role of a "talent agency" focused on aggressively *identifying and seeking* new talent—versus the old approach of screening talent that happened to come to them. Based on the profile of the skills needed, they now had to find new staff members through unconventional means—such as discovering people who might not even be in the market and convincing them to join the ranks of their company. And their biggest recruitment tool? The new vision.

When your company is propelled by a compelling vision of *what can be*—one in which all employees understand their role and how what they do matters—you will be assured that, as futurist John Schaar said, "The future is not some place we are going, but rather one we are creating. The paths are not to be found, but made, and the activity of making them changes both the maker and the destination."

In that world, nothing should be left to chance.

Five questions you should ask yourself about Vision:

1. Can each of your employees describe the company vision? Do they know how their daily activities connect to its achievement (in other words, can they "see themselves" in it)?

2. Do you hold your leadership teams accountable for the regular communication of your vision to all employees?

3. Do your functional areas specifically build their strategies and organize to drive the achievement of the vision?

4. Do you share your vision with all stakeholders? Use it in client presentations or to recruit key employees? In the on-boarding process? In front of analysts or investors?

5. Have you intentionally designed your vision to be a competitive advantage in your market, actively sharing it with your customers and clients to distinguish your organization?

Case Study

WESTERN WATER WORKS SUPPLY COMPANY

"Western Water Works Supply Company, Inc. is a distributor of waterworks materials and products that are used in the transmission of potable water."

—from the Company Profile

Joe: Let's get this fully in perspective; Western Water Works Supply Company is the oldest pipe, valve, and fitting distributor in the state. It's a pipe company. In the age of Internet, whiz kid businesses, it's about as unglamorous a case study as you can come up with—that is, unless you consider a very long track record of performance and extraordinary customer loyalty to be the ultimately glamorous position in business . . . which I do.

With all of the books and articles about the wonders of doing business in our brave new hyper-connected world, it's easy to overlook a company as seemingly mundane as a pipe distributor in Chino, California. But that would be a mistake. Western Water Works Supply Company might just be one of the best places around to learn how a business—*any* business—is supposed to work.

I first learned of the company after they had read a few of my books and contacted me about coming to work with them and some of their top customers about the principles therein. I've crossed paths with hundreds of companies of all kinds and sizes in my consulting and speaking work. Occasionally, a company will stand out for one reason or another; and this was one of those occasions. Chuck, Kris, and I have focused this book on ideas from companies that truly "get" how to align people and strategy through intentional leadership. Western Water Works "gets it"; boy, do they get it.

And I'm not the only one who feels that way. My good friend—author and speaker Mark Sanborn (*The Fred Factor, The Encore Effect*)—also agrees that Western Water Works exhibits a unique quality of leadership. I asked Mark to share his thoughts about the company, and here's what he had to say:

> Businesspeople love data, [which] regrettably causes them to miss some key insights into organizations. One of the things I look for when I work with a company is energy: How engaged, involved, and energized are the people who work there? Western Water Works may well set the bar for that decidedly soft but important measure.
>
> The energy and engagement are palpable. People aren't going through the motions; they are enjoying their work, their colleagues, and being of service to the customer.

That kind of energy comes from a truly unique culture where people are carefully selected for their jobs and then developed, encouraged, rewarded, and appreciated. [People at] Western Water Works . . . exemplify those who don't just go to work to make money; their work also gives them a chance to make meaning.

This company is a classic example of one whose decisions and actions are driven by a clearly articulated and constantly discussed vision—"To become the primary waterworks supplier to the premier underground contractors and water utilities"—as well as a set of well-worn, "this is how we do it" values—"Discipline, Innovation, Integrity, Professionalism."

It's not that there's magic in the above words; rather, the magic is in their daily use and the fact that these words drive what happens every day, all day long. Everything at Western Water Works is done with a singular goal in mind: to create a loyal customer. The vision and values are the road map that are faithfully referenced and followed at all times. Western Water Works is a classic example of alignment of people and strategy through intentional leadership.

Of everything that the company does right—and that covers a lot of territory—the most impressive to me may well be their Discipline value: "The right people in the right positions who are free to act while following defined processes; a rigorous push towards results, one step at a time." With the ultimate goal of creating loyal customers, the employees of Western Water Works are not simply people who are very good at their jobs (which they most assuredly are). They are imbued with the vision and values, which they then turn loose to create opportunities and solve problems for customers *on the spot*. Much like renowned high-end hotel chain Ritz Carlton, Western Water Works Supply has emphasized the importance of and responsibility for customer satisfaction throughout the entire organization; and, most importantly, it has empowered employees to take action.

Western Water Works is a learning organization. From their emphasis on seeking innovative ways to prevent and solve customer problems, to their devotion to personal development, this company wants every member to grow and become better at what they do. As one employee says, "One reason I like working here is because the company has people that are willing to help you become better."

And the company's interest in constant personal improvement isn't limited to their own employees; they want to spread the education around. The Western Water Works website has a "Personal Development" page that not only lists recommended books, but it also provides links to Amazon.com so that website visitors can easily buy them.

To gain more insight into the practice of intentional leadership at Western Water Works Supply Company, I asked some questions of Bruce Himes, President.

Joe: You focus heavily on your vision and values. It seems to be part of your everyday conversation, rather than just something you pull out for meetings. How important are these in terms of how you do business day to day?

Bruce: That could be a book in itself. Our vision and values are two parts of our four-part mission statement, which are our purpose, values, vision (goals), and top three objectives. Taken together, this is what we are about.

Our purpose defines "why" we do what we do. It is our emotional driver. Our core values are what underlie our beliefs; these values form a template from which we make all decisions. Our core values also serve as a great checks-and–balances device to keep us strong and flexible. Processes and strategies may change to suit different situations and environments (flexibility); but we can always rely upon our values to provide consistency (strength).

Perhaps even more importantly, our values help us to determine which types of people need to be and stay on our team. This is critical, because we are only as good as the people in our company. While knowledge and skills can be learned, core values tend to reside deeply inside of people and are difficult to change. A person's core values can fairly accurately predict their future behavior. Our vision represents that which propels our business and keeps us focused on "where" we are going, while also clearly stating "when" we will get there. Our top three objectives—combined with our core values—let us know which critical "actions" we need to take daily to achieve our purpose and vision.

Joe: You seem to empower employees to be innovative and take responsibility for heading off or solving customer problems on the spot. How important is that in your quest for customer loyalty?

Bruce: First of all, creating loyal customers is our number one objective. You just cannot have a business that sustains itself and grows without loyal customers.

Second, it is easy to empower or trust people who share the same set of core values, since we have confidence in how they will respond in real time. It is our responsibility as leaders to provide our people with the right resources (tools, knowledge, and skills) and proper training so that they possess and can utilize the capabilities to solve customer challenges. This is all about our second top objective: developing others.

We also realize that our customers deal with our front-line people every day; and that loyalty is best created by and through people. Our employees are in the best position to get to know a customer, become closer to the customer than anyone else, and to connect emotionally with the customer (sound familiar, Joe?). Customer loyalty therefore begins with our ability to establish, build, and maintain relationships with our customers. Loyal customers are a natural outcome of uniting solid relationships with real value (meeting expectations) in the marketplace.

Joe: What do you look for when hiring new employees?

Bruce: We are in debt to *Good to Great* author Jim Collins for this; we look for four key things:

1. Do they share our core values?
2. Do they need to be managed or led? The right people do not need to be managed; instead, they want to be led.
3. Do they have the potential to be the best in our industry and market at their position? We look at three areas when assessing a person's potential: ambition, ability, and attitude. Ambition tells us what they are *willing* to do; ability tells us what they *can* do; and attitude tells us *how* they will do it.
4. Do they know the difference between a "job" and a "responsibility"? We want people who view their role as a responsibility to accomplish our purpose, vision, and top three objectives.

Joe: You've got a relatively young management and leadership team. Is that by design? And if so, how do you develop your future leaders?

Bruce: Well, thank you for calling us young; and yes, it is by design. You are aware how important culture is to us; and although we've been in business since 1945, we have found it best to start with people as early as possible in their careers, since they haven't yet acquired bad habits and practices. Developing future leaders begins by bringing people into our company who match the four key criteria above. However, they still need coaching and mentoring (leadership). Besides training on industry-specific issues, we develop others as follows.

First, we constantly remind our people what is important (purpose, values, vision, and top three objectives). We try to do this by example, using company newsletters to highlight examples of our people living our core values—and any other method like inspirational quotes and stories that support any part of our mission statement that we send out to our staff.

Next, we have identified a core set of personal development and business books that we encourage our people to read. We have group meetings where everyone gets an opportunity to share what they are reading, learning, and changing in their behavior to improve. This is powerful stuff, and it puts employees on an equal level. Everyone gets an opportunity to be a teacher and student. We have even had some of our people form their own reading groups where they meet early in the morning to read together. Wow!

Finally, we meet one-on-one with our people on a monthly, semi-monthly, or quarterly basis, depending upon their role in our company. We help the individual discover their own definition for success and strive to connect it with our own. We also help them to identify their potential strength themes. We feel that people will grow the most by capitalizing on what they feel they're best at. In each one-on-one, we identify three action items or practices to bring them closer to their definition for success. We generally seek to identify something that they need to stop doing, start doing, and/or continue doing.

Joe: You recommend business books on your website and even provide links to buy them. Why?

Bruce: Innovation is one of our four core values, and we define it as stimulating progress. We believe that one of the best ways to inspire people to progress on a personal level is to get them to read good books on a consistent basis. Earl Nightingale said, "If you will spend an extra hour each day of study in your chosen field, you will be a national expert in that field in five years or less." Hopefully, we have identified some of the best books that support our mission statement and will help our people to achieve their own personal greatness. We also post these books on our website for our customers because we want them to progress and become more innovative as well.

Joe: You do something pretty unusual for your industry— the learning conferences you have for a club that you have created from among your top customers. I had the honor of participating in your first one. Why do you do those?

Bruce: In our efforts to stimulate progress with ourselves and our customers, we hold an annual customer conference for some of our top customers. Their purpose is to help our customers grow and improve. We figure that one of the best ways to develop our business is to help our customers develop theirs.

This idea came to us while reading your books *Becoming a Category of One* and *Indispensable*. Consequently, you were our very first speaker; and we followed you with Mark Sanborn the following year. The enthusiastic feedback we received from our customers and vendors has been overwhelming. These customer conferences have greatly enhanced our image in the industry and created significant loyalty with our customers.

Joe: Western Water Works seems to be very intent on creating loyal customers. Do you think that that's the key to sustaining success and growing as a company? And what is the key to creating loyal customers?

Bruce: Creating, building, and maintaining loyal customers may be the best way to sustain and grow a company. To us, it is the only way; and the first key to doing this is by, as I mentioned before:

1. Knowing more about the customer than anyone else.
2. Getting closer to the customer than anyone else.
3. Connecting emotionally to the customer.

The other key is to provide real value; and this means that we are helping the customer improve financially or strategically. In other words, we help them enhance their competitive advantage.

Joe: If you were to give advice to someone starting a business today, what would that advice be?

Bruce: Get clear on your purpose or your "why" for what you do. Discover your core values. Have a deep and simple understanding on what it is that you provide the marketplace that your customer cannot get anywhere else. Set a vision that defines where you are going and when you will get there. Finally, determine the top three objectives that will accomplish your vision. We suggest that they be:

1. Creating loyal customers.
2. Developing your people.
3. Achieving best in the class business performance.

I think what's truly remarkable about Western Water Works Supply Company is that they don't do anything that *any* of us couldn't do. It's not that their ideas are so radically innovative or noteworthy; it's that they are so disciplined, and that they do the right things day in and day out. They have, quite simply, chosen to do the things that create success. Why wouldn't any of us choose to do the same?

2

Culture As a Competitive Advantage

YOU CAN'T NOT HAVE A CULTURE

Chuck: Every company has a culture. As a matter of fact, a company *can't not* have a culture. The only question is whether it is purposely and intentionally designed with a clear outcome in mind, or if it is merely an aggregation of disparate behaviors and beliefs simply left to chance—a situation where every individual employee decides how they should behave and what values they should adhere to.

A powerful and effective culture is an outcome grounded in conscious, critical thinking rather than an unintended circumstance of neglect or apathy. Developed well, a strong culture can be the bridge between the daily harsh realities of business and the human part of the organization—the context for *how* we do *what* we do. Companies who "get this" recognize that culture is a potential asset to be leveraged in a very tangible way against their competition. As such, they dedicate time determining exactly how to make this happen.

WHAT'S YOUR STORY?

Joe: Another way of looking at culture is to think of it quite simply as your "story." The benefits of having a great story begin inside, with your employees, in ways that let them not only understand but also help create it. When your people take part in creating the story every day, they internalize it. It's incorporated into everything they do and they begin to tell that story through their words, their attitudes, and every interaction with customers.

Tapping into the power of an intentional culture produces countless benefits. When you know who you are, and can consistently and effectively tell that story, you see a boost in employee morale, increased buy-in, and better attitudes. This isn't a temporary effect from a "feel-good program"; rather, it's an ongoing, always-growing improvement in how your employees feel about themselves and their work. When employees understand how they fit into a story that they genuinely feel a part of, then everything they do takes on a new significance and purpose. And work with purpose becomes meaningful work.

Another great benefit of a clear, intentional culture is that you naturally begin to attract the employees that you want. Without clarity of culture, how in the world would potentially great staff know they want to work with you? Extraordinary companies attract employees with qualities that fit the uniqueness of the brand. But adopting an intentional culture doesn't mean taking a cookie-cutter approach to people. Part of that culture may very well be diversity in many forms, including diversity of opinion. Within that diversity, however, everyone knows who they are and what's important to the team.

Obviously, when you attract the right people as employees, who then live and embody your story, you begin to reach customers, potential customers, and even vendors and partners in ways that you otherwise could not have. The experience of "what it's like" to do business with you becomes a driving force in why people choose to. The experience that you create through culture—through every customer touch point and personal interaction—becomes your greatest competitive differentiator.

HOW SHOULD WE BEHAVE?

Chuck: In many cases, culture is too often left to chance and thought to represent an intangible or "soft asset" that will take care of itself "if we just hire good people and point them in the right direction." Organizations that intentionally develop and leverage their culture generate more value than companies who do not. They don't see culture as an interesting by-product of people who work together; rather, they consider it to be a critical resource in delivering their vision. In essence, culture is the result of "vision back" thinking: How do we intentionally design a culture that will enable the vision to be realized more quickly and more effectively?

Some years ago during a strategic planning session, a new member of our executive leadership team made this point simply and beautifully by asking, "How should we behave among ourselves and in front of our clients in order to make our vision a reality?" The question was met with an uncomfortable and resounding silence (and my silence was as embarrassingly loud as anyone on our team). Up to this point, we had viewed our culture as a collection of everything that had preceded us in the decades-old company we were leading. While we knew we were its stewards, we had not actively asked ourselves this important question, or even thought about rethinking this asset in this framework. After those first clumsy moments of silence, it broke loose. I'm not certain I had ever seen a more engaged and energetic conversation among my team.

This launched us into the process of auditing our culture in an entirely new context. We moved from the care and feeding of the old, passively accepted legacy culture to one that we actively created to distinguish us from our competition. We realized that our limited thinking had been self-imposed, and we now had a new question before us: How could we, as company leaders, leverage culture as an asset we could align to support our strategy and vision? If we were intent upon achieving the new plan we had developed, then why assume that the old culture, left untouched, would automatically be as useful in the new world as it was in the old? Answer: It wouldn't.

Does that mean we ripped it all up and threw it away? Of course not. There were some critical aspects of the heritage that became foundational elements of our new vision. There were also new elements that needed to be integrated in order to execute our redefined future. If we did not take the responsibility to act against this, who would? It was clear to us that cultural design started at the top as one of the key obligations of our leadership team. Our strong performance here would catalyze our organization. If we chose to overlook it, it was not the type of thing that an organization, especially a large one, could achieve at a grass-roots level. We knew that we needed to take responsibility for what we might lose if we failed to act against this. All of this, stemming from one simple question.

CULTURE ALIGNED WITH VISION

The process became incredibly engaging, and the activity was almost maniacal. Our focus was to purposefully align culture with our vision because, while we knew that products and services could be deconstructed, reverse engineered, and replicated, we were convinced that a culture we could leverage in the marketplace could be a significant advantage that could not be copied. It had the "secret sauce" elements that true competitive advantage is made of and we were obligated to use every tool at our disposal to win in our market.

The benefits of this work extended well beyond re-architecting our culture. It drove incredible engagement among employees, clients, and shareholders, and redefined our approach to the market. It also became clear that much of our work was easily transferred across our own business divisions, as well as the industry we served. In many cases, clients contacted us and asked that we do for them "what we had done" with our culture. In two years, we had over 1,100 client executives visit our new call center to learn about our culture, our process for designing it, and how it made us a more strategic and valuable partner for them.

CULTURE AS A SET OF LEADERSHIP BEHAVIORS

Joe: What characteristics should you seek and develop in your organization's leaders? The answer is in your culture. Culture isn't just a static way of being; it should also be centered on goals and aspirations. It's how you want your customers and employees to think of you. Your leaders should embody the qualities that you want in the organization.

Vision and culture are—or certainly should be—inseparable. Your culture—what you are and want to be known for—should translate into a set of leadership behaviors that propel the organization as a whole to fulfill the vision. Which of the following managerial habits and skills would help create a culture that would fulfill your organization's vision?

- managing costs effectively
- managing logistics
- customer centric
- communicating effectively
- driving innovation and creativity
- meeting deadlines
- collaborative
- solving problems quickly
- managing quality processes
- developing customer trust

It's a reciprocal formula: Your culture creates leadership, and your leadership fosters your culture. It's a matter of whether your leadership matches your vision and your culture, which must be the case if you are to create and sustain success.

ACCELERATE THE DELIVERY
OF THE STRATEGIC VISION

Chuck: What we often see in the companies we've led is that, when a culture is purposefully designed with a clear outcome in mind, it becomes an asset that can *accelerate* the delivery of the strategic vision—and the achievement of the business strategy. There is a shared orientation and belief system among companies that succeed in this alignment:

1. First and foremost, they never define the work as an "HR issue." It is instead clearly seen for what it is: a business

strategy and execution issue requiring attention from top leadership. This is a fundamental belief among the organizations that get the most return for their effort here.

2. The culture must be linked to an outcome beyond itself—namely, the strategic vision. The question becomes, "How could we behave toward ourselves and our clients in a manner that would help us realize our vision faster?" This means auditing their existing culture to see it not only for what it is, but for what it can become. Then they go to work on the gap.

3. They define culture as one of management's key obligations and realize that this initiative must start with them and that it cannot merely be delegated. The leadership team is aware that, although the rest of the organization will follow their lead, they first expect to see their leaders behaving differently. In essence, they believe that what Gandhi said is in fact true: "You must be the change you wish to see in the world."

4. They know the work is hard, and when they decide to undertake it, they never settle for building a "middle of the bell curve" culture. This is the time to establish the highest standards because, in order to gain a competitive advantage from a cultural change, it must be highly visible to clients, shareholders, and competitors—and, equally as important, to every one of their employees. They know that everyone wants to be associated with an organization that pushes itself to deliver all they are capable of doing. McDonald's founder Ray Kroc put it beautifully when he said, "The quality of a leader is

reflected in the standards they set for themselves." So become known for your standards. This level of clarity and aspiration both engages employees and can be a self-selection tool for those who aren't sure if they are up to the challenge. It's not an issue of a good versus bad choice, but rather the *right* choice for each individual. The wrong outcome is a level of uncertainty or gray area that doesn't allow employees to understand what the organization stands for and what their personal role will be in supporting that.

5. They determine how to "showcase" their culture. By rethinking their client touch points in new and creative ways, they create opportunities to make their culture not only visible but also palpable to their clients. This becomes the source of incredible employee engagement and pride because staff members see how they are inextricably linked to something they directly control—which then becomes a key reason that clients choose to do business with them instead of their competition.

Our leadership team learned the value of this lesson in a business-to-business company I led that was at a strategic crossroad. Our core product had come under intense pricing pressure in part due to the historical industry distribution strategy where our products were sold through our clients' reps to the end consumers of our product. This had been the standard for over 90 years.

We decided to change those rules and felt we could sell more of our product at higher margins *and* identify opportunities for our clients to sell more of *their* core products if we talked directly to our clients' customers, "on their behalf." This shifted our client acquisition strategy from one based on our core (but rapidly commoditizing) plant production competencies to our new sales and relationship ability in our call centers. Where we used to showcase our tangible production assets, we now had to showcase our newly designed culture to drive our competitive distinction. In essence, to take an intangible asset like culture and create a tangible, value-adding resource.

Our goal when a prospective client entered our call centers was for them to *feel* exactly what it would be like when their customers interacted with us. Every part of the environment was designed to highlight our "on behalf" culture. Each client visit and tour allowed them to participate in employee team meetings and interact with our agents, sales trainers, and team leaders. But by far the most effective strategy was letting them choose to sit with one of our 300 agents, put on a headset, and listen in live to *unscripted* conversations with *their* customers. Risky? At times. Effective? Incredibly. We wanted the ultimate display of how our culture could help them succeed in their own business, thereby distinguishing us from our competition.

The finest day our leadership ever enjoyed in terms of validating the changes we had made to our culture came after a two-hour tour of our call center with the fourth-largest bank (at the time) in the United States. After spending almost 40 minutes on the phone listening to one of our agents talk to their customers, we returned to the conference room with the EVP and his team for our debrief and presentation. When we sat down, I could see that our guest looked concerned, and I could tell our team was nervous about what he might have experienced. Perhaps this was one of those times where things had not gone as we had planned. After sitting down, I said, "Bill, you look concerned about something. Was there something we did on the tour that was a problem?" He was quiet for a moment and then said, "To tell you the truth, I am a bit concerned." I could see the blood draining from our call center leader's face. "I'm certain if you tell us what's bothering you, we can take care of whatever it is," I offered. "I don't think you can," he responded slowly. I thought the center leader was going to pass out at this point; but then Bill continued, "I'm concerned because, based on what I have seen today, it seems that your company actually treats *our* customers better than *we* treat our customers. How have you developed the type of culture to do that? Not only is this is exactly the type of partnership we have been looking for, we believe you could help us improve our own culture."

Stunned silence, followed by an audible collective sigh from our team. We had been courting this client for years and just realized that, despite everything we had done in the past, our ability to showcase and make tangible the purposeful changes we had made in our culture is what finally won them over.

6. A level of attention and willingness to "systematize" the environment, by making it an integral part of their performance review process (meaning not just measuring *what* was done, but *how* it was done), their on-boarding process and recruiting process (showcasing the culture to prospective employees through recruiters, search firms, college campuses, etc.). In addition, they create an internal language that provides a common understanding of how to talk about the culture, support it,

and internalize it so that everyone, not just the leadership team, can participate.

7. As tough as this can be, they address cultural mis-alignment issues swiftly and decisively, which makes it unacceptable to simply deliver the *what* (quantifiable objectives) without considering the *how* (cultural boundaries and behaviors). Famed GE executive Jack Welch spoke explicitly about this in terms of the "four quadrants" of performance: First, those who get results, *and* do so within the cultural guidelines, are the easiest. These are the "stars" in your organization that should be promoted and held as models of behavior and performance.

The second group is comprised of those who neither operate within the culture nor deliver the results accordingly. The disposition for this group is equally straightforward in that they are best suited to seek opportunities in other organizations where they can best thrive.

The third group—those who clearly understand the culture and the values but are not delivering the results as you wish—deserve your guidance and coaching for a determined period of time in order to bring their contributions more closely in line with the first group.

The last group is by far the most difficult to reconcile. However, it is also the most closely watched by everyone in the organization in terms of how the leaders deal with or tolerate them. These are the people who deliver results but who do so at a clear cost to the values and culture of the organization. They "break a lot of china" or "leave a trail of bodies" along the way toward achieving their goals. Their "I got it done, didn't I; so what's the problem?" approach must be dealt with directly in an organization that's serious about maintaining an ethical and value-centered culture that can be visible to clients and shareholders. Swift and certain reconciliation of troublesome cultural behavior—even in the face of positive results—must be clear and evident. Otherwise, all of the energy and communication about what the culture is and stands for will be wasted, and the toll on the leadership capital will be great as well.

8. The leaders of these companies get in front of everyone and talk about this all of the time. They love nothing more than to talk about how the culture of the company makes them distinct in their markets. They develop ways to recognize, celebrate, and tell success stories about their culture in order to make them more real, breathe life into them, and give real working examples of what it looks like when it is done well. They use these opportunities to cement the notion of "this is how we do what we do."

A HOLISTIC APPROACH TO DOING BUSINESS

Joe: From a strictly competitive perspective, there is no advertising or marketing program that can compete with a clear, intentional culture. At the same time, any advertising or marketing program that is *part of* a powerful culture becomes infinitely more effective (Exhibit A: Apple). Having an intelligible culture that's led by a clear vision is a holistic approach to doing business and a way to combine everything you do under one guiding light. It's an organizing principle that eliminates confusion and competing messages and brings clarity through shared values.

What are the sources of a company's culture? How do you begin to articulate who you are and what's important? The foundation, of course, is your vision. The way you live the vision—what you do every day, all day long, and how you do it—becomes your culture. There are a number of places to look for inspiration, including:

- **Our history**. "We've been making the greatest peppermint stick candy on the planet for over 200 years."
- **A strong point of view**. A sense of passion for what you do can be the basis for your culture. For example, there's a high-end bicycle shop in North Carolina that wins customers for its very expensive competitive products with the story of "Nobody loves bicycles more than we do." A simple statement of strong belief and love for what you do can be the basis for a compelling story.
- **Serving a larger purpose**. There are companies whose stories are built around saving people money (Dollar General Stores) or the good that comes from making the Internet more useable to everyone (Google).
- **Integrity**. "We do the right thing for our employees, our customers, and our community. The quality of the relationship is what counts the most."

Whatever the sources of inspiration for your culture are, they must ring true with all constituencies, including employees, vendors, partners, customers, shareholders, and the community at large. Designing a culture isn't about making up slogans, slapping them on banners and cards, and hoping that they'll stick. If your stated culture doesn't match what happens in the real world, then you've merely created a culture of dishonesty. And if your culture is in conflict with the vision, then you have a system that simply won't work. It would be like trying to put diesel fuel in a gasoline engine; it just won't run like it should. When it comes to culture, you can't fool any of the people any of the time.

I worked with a company years ago that had a major advertising campaign built around the slogan "Where people come first." The conflict was that the culture at this company was one of following their "cut costs" policy at the expense of customers. The more customers they lost from poor service, the more they tried to cost-cut their way back to a positive bottom line. The only group that rolled their collective eyes more than the customers at the insanely bogus "Where people come first" campaign were the employees because they were treated with even less regard than customers were. The culture spoke so loudly that no one could even hear the advertising campaign.

A COMMITMENT TO CONSISTENCY

One of the most significant challenges to sustaining a clear, intentional culture is growth. It's one thing to consistently "live" your story when you only have 12 employees; but as 12 becomes 1,200, you must vigilantly protect your story's integrity. The growth of famed coffee shop Starbucks, for instance, has been extraordinary by any measure. But with that growth came the challenge of staying true to the company's story. In January of 2008 a memo from Starbucks chairman Howard Schultz to upper management delivered a stern warning about the danger of straying from their story. Schultz lamented that rapid growth has "led to the watering down of the Starbucks experience," and that most of the company's stores "no longer have the soul of the past."

The greatest challenge that you will face in terms of your story isn't creating it; it's preserving it. How do you remain true to who you say you are and what you claim to be important? And how do you take that commitment to consistency beyond the management level and down to every employee in every department of the organization? The answer is incredibly simple and yet extremely challenging. It's found in two factors: people and repetition.

It starts with people; and you hire and develop the ones who "fit" your story. You can't mandate values or personalities through training or the company manual. For example, The Container Store hires people who love to help other people. Southwest Airlines hires people who are fun and have a sense of humor. Tractor Supply Company hires people who love the rural lifestyle.

Even people who fit and believe in your culture need support. Strong companies believe in the power of repetition, and they work at their culture every day. It's not something that they relegated to an obligatory mention at the monthly meeting. Vision drives strategy; and culture is where and how you live that vision and execute the strategy.

One final component of successfully creating and sustaining your culture is the ability to change and remain relevant to your market while staying true to your culture. To maintain its integrity, a company must remain true to its values.

Southwest Airlines founder Herb Kelleher always said that the intangibles are the hardest thing for a competitor to imitate and the most important asset to preserve. He pointed out that you can buy airplanes, negotiate for ticket counter space, and order baggage conveyors. But Kelleher felt that Southwest Airlines' spirit was the company's most valuable and hardest to imitate feature. He often said that his greatest concern was that they might lose that very special culture.

THE GUIDING FOUNDATION

Chuck: When all is said and done, your culture is the guiding foundation for how your organization—and all of its employees—work to achieve your vision. You can choose to shape your organization's culture or something else will. It is the soul of your company; do not leave it to chance.

Five questions you should ask yourself about Culture:

1. Have you answered the question, "What type of culture do we need to in order to make our vision become a reality?"
2. How do you showcase your culture to customers to gain competitive advantage?
3. Does the executive leadership team actively own the ongoing management of your culture?
4. Do you measure how employees and customers perceive your culture and understand what makes your culture distinct as a place to work and do business?
5. Do you "hire and fire" with your culture in mind, embedding it in your recruitment and performance appraisal process?

Case Study

KOWALSKI'S MARKET

Chuck: "We are teachers, not just employers," says Kris Kowalski Christiansen, COO of Woodbury, Minnesota-based Kowalski's market. Not the type of thing you hear from most grocery store operating officers; but then again, Kowalski's is not like most grocery stores. If you want to see how a powerful culture can be used to create real competitive advantage, look no further than this Minnesota grocer.

Jim and Mary Anne Kowalski founded the store following a conversation with some friends on the front porch of their home in 1983. They were talking about the need for an intimate, customer-centered, and quality-oriented grocer in their neighborhood. They realized that, if they didn't do it themselves, it simply wouldn't get done. And, as they say, the rest was history—as the humble one store has grown into a 1,200-employee, 9-location chain that reinvests over 75 percent of its profit back into store operating and continuous design improvements.

Kris Young: The fact that Jim and Mary Anne met with people in the surrounding community to find out what was important to *them* in a neighborhood market is truly inspirational. How great would it be if more business owners thought this way? What a beautiful approach: Let's find out what matters most to our customers and then make *that* the foundation of our business. What makes Kowalski's remarkable is not so much *what* they do, but *how* they do it.

Chuck: One of the things you first notice upon walking into Kowalski's is the culture. You can actually feel it. Kris and the rest of the Kowalski leadership team have continued their parents' philosophy of "people before profits". Which people? Everyone: customers, employees, even members of the community who may not even shop there. How, you might wonder, can a store affect the people who don't even visit it? It's because Kowalski's identity statement (yes, a grocery store with an identity statement) defines them as a civic organization with a commitment to run their business for the common good of the communities in which they live and work. Every employee undergoes training to learn exactly what role they play in making this happen. Additionally, Kowalski's leaders undertake 12 weeks of operating principle training, since they are the ones who must model and perpetuate the culture throughout the organization.

Kris believes that Kowalski's obligation to the community is to prepare the young people who work there to be better citizens and to learn to think for themselves. "We know that we are many of our young people's first job; and if we teach them well, it helps us as well as our community. We want them to work for us as long as they can; but if and when they do leave, we want to make certain they have a good foundation for their next employer."

Kris Young: It seems that any parent would have been thrilled to have their son or daughter work at Kowalski's and experience the training and leadership modeled there. However, beyond the training the most important thing Kowalski's does for their employees—particularly the younger ones—is to believe in them. This company believes there is a leader in each one of their employees; and, more importantly, they tell them so. Each employee is expected to play a valuable role in their customer's experience and in the business's success. Simply put, Kowalski's hires leaders; and they teach them that leadership doesn't stop when you leave the workplace.

Chuck: It's very clear that Kowalski's made a decision from the start to design a culture with a clear vision to serve others—and, as a result, distinguish themselves in their markets and develop a competitive advantage. What began as a small enterprise intended to fill the gap of a market that was truly focused on its customers has remained to this day. All decisions are made with the customer in mind—from the first feedback session on Jim and Mary Anne's front porch to the constant focus groups they conduct with customers in every store.

One of the most appealing things about the culture is that it is grounded in reality and simplicity. I asked Kris what criterion they used to make decisions about how they wanted their culture to "show up" in front of their customers and she said, "It's not that scientific. We simply think about how we like to be treated when we do business somewhere."

Can it really be that simple? It can be, if you really listen, act on the information you get from customers, and then teach your employees how they *matter* in executing on their behalf. You witness this every time you are in one of Kowalski's stores—whether you are a first time guest or a committed customer.

The stores are absolutely beautiful, impeccably clean, and filled with the highest quality items. Kris told us that Kowalski's realizes that, while groceries are their life, shopping for them can be a boring task for most people; so they reinvest to continually upgrade their store designs and aesthetics. She shared that, while this helps the customer experience, they also know their employees perform better working in an inviting, clean, and visually appealing environment. They believe a great customer experience begins with a great employee experience. And they're right.

Need an item that's not in stock? Just ask, and they'll get it for you. If it's an unusual item, they'll negotiate a special rate on a case for you so you can have a supply of it at home and not have to search each time you need it. Try to get through check out with a carton of eggs, produce, or other perishable without the checker making certain nothing is broken or bruised. If anything is, a replacement is delivered lightening quick to the register so as not to delay the checkout process.

Need help to the car with your bags? You don't even need to ask; it's part of the service they provide. Can't find an item? An employee will stop whatever they are doing to walk you directly to where it is on the shelves. Have an idea that would help them serve you better? A manager will be with you in seconds to listen to what you have to say. Want to have part of your purchase price go to charity? Simply drop your receipt into one of a dozen slots representing local organizations on your way out the door, and they'll make that happen.

Want to tip the carryout person for getting your groceries to your car on a brutally cold and wintry Minnesota day? Forget it, no tipping allowed. I tried to do this the first time I shopped there, only to have the 16-year-old young man who helped me say, "No thank you, sir. We don't take tips; we just want to make certain you and your groceries get to the car in good shape. We appreciate you shopping with us."

Kris Young: Chuck's not kidding. In fact, every single time I shop there I am surprised by the conversation one of those young people will start on our way out to my car. I often think, "This could be one of the most pleasant conversations I've had all day. This young person is well mannered, helpful, and utterly charming." When I get in my car and drive away I smile because I realize they did it again.

Kowalski's makes a big impression simply by doing a lot of things right. Their stores are aesthetically pleasing, neighborhood markets focused on high quality and impeccable customer service. In other words, they have their core business nailed. This is largely due to a culture built on listening to customers, respecting them, and then executing with the pure and focused approach they have to running their business. Kris Kowalski ends our discussion by summing it up so simply: "It's just what we do. We wouldn't know how to think any differently."

3

RELEVANCE

Does Your Company Matter?

THE MOST IMPORTANT COMPETITIVE QUESTION

Joe: Famed business leader Peter Drucker is credited for saying that the purpose of business is to create and keep a customer; and if there is one idea that's central to creating and keeping customers, it is relevance. The most important competitive question you can ask about your company is, "How relevant are we to our customers?" As long as your customers find you relevant to them, their businesses, success, and lives, then you will prosper and grow. You don't merely align people and strategy as an exercise in organizational development; there's a point to it. And the point, as Drucker claims, is to produce and keep customers.

I travel quite a bit for work, and my schedule on the road is extremely hectic. So when I'm at home, I take great pleasure in having a morning routine. It's comforting during these days of chaotic travel to have some things that keep me grounded. One important part of my routine is to go out every morning for a cup of coffee; and I always go to the Starbucks in the

Green Hills Mall near my home office. There's another coffee shop just a few doors down, and it's actually really great. In my opinion, the coffee is about as good as Starbucks', and the pastries are actually much better.

So why do I go to Starbucks? Well, Starbucks has the *New York Times*, and the other coffee shop has *USA Today*; and while *USA Today* is a fine newspaper, I really love and prefer to read the *New York Times*. Starbucks wins when it comes to creating the total experience that I want as a customer—not with coffee, but with the newspaper that they carry. It makes them more relevant to me.

What can this little story possibly have to do with you and your customers? Everything. As a leader, relevance is one of the lenses through which you should use to make every decision, every single day. Does this decision advance the vision and fit our culture? Does this decision make us more relevant to our customers? The question of relevance is especially vital from a competitive standpoint. You compete to the extent that you are relevant to your customers, and you differentiate to the extent that you are more relevant than your competition.

A Fortune 500 company for whom I did some work had always focused on product quality as its primary differentiator. During the recession of 2009, the company's leaders were exploring how to capture market share from competitors that they sensed were "hunkered down" and riding out the economic situation. Rather than assume that product quality would be their ticket to acquiring new business, they decided to ask their customers what was most important to them right at that moment—and what they discovered surprised them.

It turned out that their customers didn't consider product quality to be a differentiator; instead, they saw it as an entry-level standard that anyone with whom they did business had to meet. Most customers deemed two factors—on-time delivery of products and flexibility of payment terms—as most important to them at the time. These competitive factors made vendors most relevant to them. You could say that on-time delivery was the equivalent to them of what the *New York Times* was to me in my earlier example. Essentially, you have to find out what makes you matter to your customers and what would make you matter even *more*. It's not optional.

So how do you find out how to be relevant to your customers? It's simple: You ask them. Your methods can range from formal market research, to having conversations, to simply paying attention. If you own a coffee shop, are you asking your customers what newspaper they would prefer? If you own an industrial supply business, are you asking your customers what they need in terms of material and delivery? *Every* employee—not just management—should be asking questions, having conversations, and looking for clues with every customer interaction they have. Part of your culture should be your constant attempt to be more relevant to customers.

THE BASIS FOR EVERY BUYING DECISION

If you analyze every buying decision for every product or service in the marketplace, a case can be made that it always comes down to relevance. What provider ultimately connects with you in a way that makes a difference? What company truly understands who you are and what's important to you? Which product or service meets both your emotional and your logical needs? You do business with the company that you determine, consciously or not, to be most relevant to you. It is the basis for every buying decision.

Consider the common factor in all of these buying decision processes:

- You are interviewing website design companies for a new business that will sell socks on the Internet. One of the design companies you are considering shows you their portfolio of clients, which includes universities, hospitals, three nonprofit organizations, a community theater, and a city government. How relevant is this company to your new business?

- You own a car repair body shop whose vision is to provide true professionalism through high-quality repair work at a relatively low price. Three different auto paint manufacturers want your business. One has the lowest price by far but lousy quality paint, while the other two have good quality paint that's comparably priced. However, one also offers its customers help with the actual operation of a business, including services on everything from managing your receivables to inventory control. Who's relevant here?

- You don't buy anything unless you feel like it's a great deal. You pride yourself on always getting the lowest price. Therefore, Wal-Mart = Relevant.

- You are a hospital CEO facing daunting challenges, including your hospital's need for a new computer system. You heard presentations from two salespeople this morning: one that focused solely on the technical capabilities of their computer systems, and the other about how to help successfully manage your hospital's current challenges and create opportunity through technology. What's the relevance here?

- You're a parent shopping for your child's first cellular phone. There's an array of products available with every feature imaginable including music, games, buzzers, and bells of every kind. However, none of this is nearly as relevant to you as your child's safety. One phone company offers a cell phone with a built-in locater device that can track your child's location with the push of a button if she were ever lost or felt as though she were in danger. *That* is relevance.

- You are a department manager tasked with deciding which employee to promote. One candidate is great at execution, while the other candidate is great at execution *and* comes up with ideas on how to increase revenue, improve customer loyalty, and reduce costs. Relevance.

- You're choosing a production company to run your annual sales meeting. Three separate groups display their brilliance in designing fabulous sets, featuring eye-popping entertainment, and creating fabulous themes for events. The fourth production company approaches you and says, "Tell us about your vision for your business and where you're trying to go with it. We want to know who you are and what's important to you because we are here to help you achieve your vision, not just stage an event. We measure our success by yours. That's what gets us up every morning." Relevance.

In all of the examples given above, consider the fact that relevance is the one thing that takes your product or service out of the commodity category and puts you squarely into a clearly differentiated competitive position. The key is to know *exactly* who your customer is and what is truly important to him or her. For me and my morning coffee ritual, it's the *New York Times*. For the industrial buyer, it may be on-time or expedited delivery. Don't make assumptions; your organization should be a nonstop, 24/7 information-gathering operation—and turn that information into relevance to the customer. That is what will then turn into business success.

A RELEVANT STRATEGY

If you were to choose one guiding principal for your business strategy, you might do well to choose relevance. Far too many companies make incredibly important, even *fundamental* decisions in a vacuum. Executives go on retreats to formulate strategy and get caught in the trap of ideas that seem "great" to them—but not to anyone who's buying. If your strategy doesn't ultimately create relevance to the client or the customer, then you are, unfortunately, irrelevant.

I'm a partner in a restaurant that opened almost 10 years ago in a neighborhood that was considered "edgy" at the time. It was one of those barely emerging urban regions, still very much off the beaten path and not a seemingly obvious choice for a restaurant location. But we believed that the area would grow and attract young homeowners and other businesses.

And, much to our delight, we were incredibly relevant here. Almost every review of the restaurant used the word "hip" to describe us. Our menu was innovative; our chef, manager, and staff were cool; and the interior was funky. We showed old, campy movies on Monday nights. We had (and still have) Stephanie, the best bartender in Nashville. The artists, musicians, and entrepreneurs moving into the neighborhood loved us. We were relevant to their lives and preferred social activities.

Flash forward to a time when the neighborhood started to change. Instead of 20-somethings dressed in all black walking down the street, we started seeing 30-something parents pushing baby carriages. Fewer people were ordering the adventurous tapas dishes from our menu. Little by little, we felt our relevance slipping away. We were "hip" in a marketplace that really wasn't looking for "hip" so much anymore. They were looking for a friendly little neighborhood bar that served great food, while we were still the edgy restaurant that had a cool bar.

INTENTIONAL LEADERSHIP— INTENTIONAL RELEVANCE

Our situation was not unusual or unique; businesses lose their relevance every day. The problem is that they don't see it coming, or even happening. Most of them don't have a clear definition of relevance or a process in place to discover or deliver it. Even as they continue to lose customers, they keep doing the same things—only harder and faster. They employ a strategy that says, "What we're doing isn't working anymore, so let's do a lot more of it." The problem is relevance; but it's also an opportunity.

Fortunately, our restaurant's leadership recognized the relevance issue and very intentionally changed our strategy accordingly. We became what our new marketplace wanted: a friendly neighborhood bar that serves great food. We've got more comfort food selections on the menu, and we've put family friendly booths inside. We took down the funky chandeliers and make the chairs cushier and more comfortable. We even put some artwork on the walls. Believe me, going from hip, bare walls to hanging something on them was a big step for us.

The first review of our new menu and format by the local daily newspaper was a home run. Rocket science? Hardly. It was just a matter of recognizing that we provided a product that, though once popular in our current location, was no longer appropriate for the market in which we now found ourselves. We deliberately reviewed our strategy from top to bottom in relation to our market. We recognized that our target patrons had moved away or that their lifestyle and/or situations had changed. We were no longer relevant, so we purposely made some significant changes.

WHAT KEEPS ME UP AT NIGHT?

Chuck: Several of the companies I've had the opportunity to lead were business-to-business organizations that provided services to other businesses. In one particular meeting several years ago, we were conducting an annual strategic review with a client where the top leaders from each company presented their respective visions and strategic plans to one another to ensure strong alignment between the two organizations. Near the end of their CEO's presentation, an interesting thing happened. A slide that was titled "What Keeps Me Up at Night" flashed across the screen. Our client's CEO quickly went past it and apologized for mistakenly including it in this presentation. I interrupted him and asked if he would mind going back to it because it had caught my attention.

The slide included a very simple list of five items. He explained that one of his board members had asked that he prepare a list outlining the key issues that he was most concerned might affect his company's future success. I mentioned to him that we had some extra time during the meeting and asked if he would mind sharing his thoughts about this list with my team— and he agreed. Quite by accident, this turned out to be the most impactful part of our meeting and served as a critical lesson for me and my team.

For the next 40 minutes, our client shared his list of concerns—as well as the potential opportunities that these issues offered—and described how he wrestled with these. I could tell by his team's reaction that even they had not seen or heard much about this. I asked what his plan was, and he admitted that it wasn't clear yet, since the market was evolving so quickly that the "standard solutions" no longer applied. He was also certain that any future plans would require new strategic partnerships, since he was not going to be able (or want) to build all of these capabilities internally. Though he had not decided who the best partners to provide that support would be, he declared that, given the magnitude of the issues, he would prefer to work with companies he knew, whose brands he respected. After finishing, he turned to me and said, "You know, I certainly can't tell you where you should take your company in the future; but I can tell you if you felt you could help us in any of these areas, you'd be one of the companies we would listen to." We finished the meeting and convened for the day.

For two days, I couldn't get his comments off my mind. It was one of those comments that gnaws at you until you do something about it. What he had essentially told us was:

1. While I like you and your company, what you guys do for me today doesn't solve the key issues at the top of my list (and by the way, here's my list).

2. I am looking for partners who can help provide solutions that will be more relevant to me and our organization in driving our future success—preferably, a company (brand) I know and trust.

3. I plan to work with these new partners personally.

I asked our leadership team members to meet with me to discuss this. We began by drawing a pyramid with six levels inside of it. The first five were our clients' list of the five issues that keep him up at night. On the sixth or lowest level, we listed the products and services that our company currently provided. As you moved up the pyramid, the issues were increasingly important and the solutions therefore more relevant. We also noted that, the closer you got to the top of the pyramid, the higher the level of executive you dealt with in their organization. In our current position we were in a mature industry that provided an increasingly commoditized offering. As a result, we found that our relationship over the years had fallen from the strategic executive level to the areas that dealt more specifically with commodity buying. It was clearly not where we wanted to be; and frankly, it was one of the most pressing items on my list of things that kept *me* awake at night.

This is not an industry-specific issue. By our definition, relevance is the value a company brings to its customers on the chief issues they face. The more vital a problem you help a customer solve, the more relevant you are to them. As my partner Joe would say, think of it as constantly trying to make yourself *indispensable*. Not a bad position to occupy in the minds of your clients and customers.

Of course, this doesn't mean that you can't run a strong business delivering a commodity product or service to clients. But for companies that wish to continue to grow their value to clients and stay ahead of the relentless march toward commoditization and price-based competition, increasing your relevance is essential.

RELEVANCE IS CHANGING AND EVOLVING

Chuck: The concept of relevance is not static; it is constantly evolving. Here are some of the things that can diminish your relevance to your customers and clients:

- **Disruptive competitors** who are not encumbered by the historic approaches to the way you and your industry work (and who have no desire or "skin in the game" to continue them).
- **Changes in technology** that affect your product or service by making it extinct, more like everyone else, or that allow more competitors into the game.
- **Shifts in buyer behavior**; for example, does the new generation of buyer care as much about what you have to offer as the previous one did?
- **Your own success**. Companies that have been perennial leaders and as such feel they know everything about their customers must be overly attentive to staying current. Specializing in *what used to matter* to your customers is a clear path to diminished relevance.
- **Company cultures** that don't value customer-centric, continuous learning approaches with their clients and customers.

It's important to realize that your customer—not you—will always determine your degree of relevance. However, left unattended, your risk of being less relevant increases exponentially. Companies who are highly relevant to their customers take a very intentional approach to understanding where they currently stand and how they can increase their worth. These organizations begin this process with clear answers to the following questions:

- Do they know their clients' businesses well enough to understand which issues directly affect their strategy's success? If not, do they have a process to gather and validate these?
- Once they have this information, they must map their existing products and services over these issues to determine: What is their current state of relevance? Do their existing products help in these areas? Do they get in the way? Or do they really matter at all? While everyone *hopes* their products are incredibly important to their customers, hope is not an effective strategy. Rather, this is the time for dispassionate, objective, fact-based thinking.
- If they are not where they want to be following this audit, how could they redeploy their assets and resources in a manner that drives success in these more important areas?
- Does their brand have *permission* to move into these new areas? In other words, how big of a leap is it for their current brand to be seen as a potential solution for these issues of higher importance? Is it an incremental alteration to the brand or a large scale brand repositioning strategy?

- Are they driving a high level of urgency around their strategy to become more relevant? Leaders who have been through this know they can never become too relevant too quickly.

WHO YOUR CUSTOMER *IS* OR WHO YOUR CUSTOMER *WAS*?

Joe: What I love about Chuck's example is that it's universal, in that his customer's issues and challenges were evolving so quickly. Here's the thing: *Everyone's* issues are evolving that quickly. Whether your customer is a bank, a car buyer, a teenager buying a new pair of jeans, or a Fortune 500 company, what they want is constantly changing.

Think about your customers specifically in terms of the number of significant life- or business-altering events that affected them over just the last two weeks. My guess is that it could be in the thousands—which means that you are dealing with different (sometimes significantly so) people or companies than you were a mere 14 days ago. How aware are you of these changes? What's your method for staying "in the know" with your customers?

Most companies' competition, markets, technology, and need for capital—amongst many, many other factors— have changed drastically of late. Consumers experience changes like the birth of children, the buying/selling/paying off of homes, toddlers becoming teens, the environment becoming a relevant buying factor, and technology like iPods ruling their households.

The point is that your customers have changed—whoever they are. They have changed since this time yesterday, and they have certainly changed *significantly* within the last year. Are you still relevant to them?

Countless businesses have strategies based on who their customers *were* instead of who they *are*. We check in with our customers once a year and think that will make us "current." We often don't realize that, by the time we leave their office or finish reading through the latest consumer survey, the information is obsolete. There was once an advertisement for an investment firm that said, "You think you understand the situation. What you don't understand is that the situation just changed." I couldn't have said it better.

All of this means that staying in touch with customers has never been more vital. You can't assume that your customers or clients will call you up and let you know when their needs change. They will much more likely simply replace you with someone who is more relevant. I believe that more customers are lost because of irrelevance than because of poor quality, high price, or bad service combined.

LISTEN AND LEARN

Chuck: Joe's comments about how important it is to stay in touch are incredibly important. As a matter of fact, this process of "checking in" is the best way to continue to audit your level of relevance and receive feedback from the best source around: your customers. Companies who clearly comprehend where they fall on their customers' relevance hierarchy use various means to continuously audit themselves. These range from formal research projects designed to specifically measure relevance, to simply holding customer meetings with this in mind.

One of the most efficient, cost-effective, and simplest ways to accomplish this is to talk to top-level executives in a setting deliberately designed for this type of discussion. The goal is to gather straightforward, actionable feedback from top-level clients and then assess and act on what is learned.

I had just become president and COO of a company and asked our sales teams to choose a top executive from 10 to 12 of their clients who they felt were the best thinkers in our industry. I sent them a letter inviting them to a dinner with us at a nice restaurant where we had set up a private dining area conducive to engaging and uninterrupted conversation. I told our teams that my goal was to find out from these top executives what *they* felt were the most pressing issues in the industry. This particular organization had never done this before and since I was new, I received some interesting feedback from my own team, which, paraphrased, sounded something like, "You know, you're new here and no one in the industry really knows you, so you probably won't get much response on this. Plus, we aren't launching a new product—so what are you going to talk about over a long dinner? Actually, *we* don't even know you that well either and are a little concerned as to what you might do in front of *our* accounts." Fair enough. But after some additional assurance on my part, we went ahead.

I opened this "pilot" dinner by saying: "As the new president of this company, I want to thank you for taking your valuable time to join us tonight. Let me share our agenda for tonight. I know several of you may be anticipating a new product or service introduction tonight; and as much as I would love to take advantage of this captive environment to do so, that's not why we asked you to join us. As a matter of fact, we don't plan to talk about *our* company tonight at all. We have been serving you in this industry for over 75 years. You have rewarded us with your business, and we are very grateful. We are committed to constantly understanding how our products and services matter in the overall scheme of the important issues you face. So tonight, I'd like to pose one question to you and ask for your feedback. Our goal is to listen and learn from our discussion, so that we can serve you even better. We would like to know what you believe to be the most difficult, the most intractable industry issues you encounter as the leaders of your organizations—those problems that consume your thoughts and keep you awake at night."

After a short (and somewhat uncomfortable) silence, one of our guests timidly said, "Well, I don't know about the rest of you, but the new regulatory environment is driving me crazy. It seems to change by the hour."

"No kidding," responded another. "I've been in this business 30 years and I've never seen anything like it. What are you guys doing at your organization to deal with this?"

Three hours later, our team had to end the dinner because the restaurant was closing. For one entirely uninterrupted evening, we had the opportunity to listen to our best clients talk about their most worrisome issues—the areas in which they were dying for not only solutions, but also partners to help them.

Needless to say, the account teams were overjoyed. Never had they seen so much valuable information come in such a free-flowing manner or looked so good for doing so little. Likewise, our VP of product development was ecstatic and couldn't take enough notes to share with his team.

Word spread that not only did we avoid a disaster in this first meeting, but we had a clear and resounding success. Requests from our sales teams to have a "Client Executive Dinner" in their areas took off. We completed 11 more of these that year, each of which was as productive as the first. We had clearly met our goals of understanding from our clients' perspective what issues concerned them the most; determined where they needed greater help; and even discovered how they saw us as a potential solution provider in these areas. What we *hadn't* expected were the other benefits:

- Of the 110 clients who attended our nine sessions, not one was lost over the course of the year to a competitor during a contract bid: 100 percent retention!
- In addition to the incredible insight we gained, over 35 of the organizations volunteered to partner with us to develop and pilot new solutions in these areas.
- Our sales people were seen in an entirely different light by the clients—and had even more access to these high-level decision makers as a result.

Was this all because we bought them a great dinner? Hardly. It was a direct outcome of demonstrating our intent to listen, learn, and commit to acting on their behalf.

KNOW MORE ABOUT THE CUSTOMER THAN ANYONE ELSE

Joe: In the almost 30 years that I have been in business, I have never wavered in this belief: Let me know more about the customer than my competition knows, and I will be positioned to win. As I look back on the ideas I've tried that didn't work—and there were a lot of them—the one thing that most of them have in common is a lack of relevance.

I've attempted a good amount of business ventures over the years that I thought were the greatest ideas since sliced bread. The problem was that the marketplace didn't agree. The ideas weren't relevant to them. That was okay, though, because each failed idea provided new information about what the market *did* want and what *would* make me relevant. This information resulted in the creation of some plans that did indeed work.

Sales success comes when you align customer needs with your own relevance to those needs. My greatest achievements in obtaining new business, or expanding existing business, always came as a result of my ability to demonstrate relevance.

I once received an email from the VP of Sales for an industrial cleaning company who wanted me to submit a proposal to consult with them on ways to increase their sales. He also informed me that he wished to schedule an initial telephone call, which we did. He opened the call by saying that, although he wasn't sure what I knew about his company, there were some changes occurring with which they needed some help. I told him that I knew that their new CEO came from an operations background, as opposed to the previous CEO's sales background. I was also aware that they were successfully emerging from bankruptcy reorganization and had completely redesigned their sales and distribution model. Another important item was that new government regulations directing the use of cleaning chemicals was their entire industry and inciting a reconsideration of the nature of the basic product and service that they offered.

At this point, I was relevant.

I went on to say that, rather than submit a proposal for consulting services at this point, I would rather fly to their headquarters and spend a day with him and others in the company who could help me gain a solid understanding of who they are, where they want to take the company, and how they hoped to get there. I'd be happy to do this on my own dime to help determine whether or not I was a good match for them. If I felt that I wasn't the best resource for their situation, I'd be happy to recommend someone who I thought would be a better fit.

At this point, I was *extremely* relevant.

He took me up on my offer, and I flew to the city where their headquarters was located. When I passed through security at the airport, my contact was there to meet me. He offered his hand and said, "Welcome, Joe. And I'm pretty sure you've got the job."

Relevance.

The real lesson for me in this experience is that merely asking and attempting to discover what can make you more relevant with customers can *in and of itself* make you more relevant. The customer then, quite naturally, waits for the payoff, which will be your responding with products or services that are relevant.

So ask yourself two questions:

1. What significant events may have taken place in the lives of my customers that I don't know about?
2. How am I going to find out what is relevant to them *now*?

Do not let your business fail to reach its potential because you got stuck doing something that you're "good at." The easiest thing in the world is to stay in your comfort zone and do what customers have always valued—only to wake up one day and find that their values and needs have drastically changed.

INTENTIONALLY CHANGE TO BECOME MORE IMPORTANT TO CUSTOMERS

Chuck: It's no secret that leaders affect their companies' worth as much by the questions they *don't* ask as by the ones they do ask. Avoiding the tough questions simply makes companies more comfortable in their current state—and violates their obligation to shareholders to continually increase their value. Seeking honest answers to these questions and using them to encourage deliberate change is what intentional leaders are all about. Introspective organizations can begin their journey to becoming more relevant by asking themselves the following questions:

- Is it increasingly difficult for our sales teams to access the top leaders and decision makers in our client organizations?
- Have we lost any business to competitors that weren't on our radar screen in the last couple of years? How did that happen?
- Are we the knowledge leaders in our industry? Do we know more about clients and customers than any competitor? If not, why? Who owns this in our organization?
- Do we find ourselves trying to increase value by "doing the old way harder" even though we are getting fewer results?

One of the most important things we've learned over the years is that companies that *intentionally intervene* against the relentless forces pushing them toward commodity status and extinction have the power to affect their destiny. There is nothing more relevant than an organization led by people who have the courage to turn themselves inside out, be honest about what they see, and then deliberately change to make themselves more important to their customers.

The longstanding wisdom still rings true: "When the rate of change on the outside exceeds the rate of change on the inside, the end is near."

Five questions to ask yourself about Relevance:

1. What process do you use to determine what matters most to your customers *now?* Do you routinely assess this process?

2. Is your product or service increasingly dealt with at lower levels in your clients' organizations as opposed to high-level decision makers? Do you talk more often about how your products are being commoditized?

3. As an organization, do you spend less time researching and learning about your customers because you have been in the business for a long time and "know everything you need to know"?

4. Are you clear on what the important issues are that your products solve from your clients' or customers' perspective? When did you last validate this?

5. Are you invited to have a "seat at the strategic table" in your clients' organizations, participating in helping them craft strategy to deal with the critical issues that go beyond your current products?

Case Study

APPLE STORES

Joe: One thing we really like about this book is that we feature a lot of relatively unknown companies. We didn't fill it with stories about the "usual suspects"—all of those companies that are at the top of every (yawn) "Best Companies" lists.

So when it came to Apple, we hesitated. So much has already been written about this brand; why would we include it in *our* book? Well, because if your book is about aligning people and strategy, as this book is, we quite simply can't *not* include Apple. Not only does the company have a history of creating incredibly innovative products; they've also reinvented the retail experience with their Apple Stores. If you haven't been to one of these locations, then immediately go—and learn.

Chuck: Apple is a great example of how to align culture, relevance, customer experience, and vision. They have a clear end stated view of technology as an empowering tool to help customers achieve what matters most to them. They know who they are and who they appeal to. They command a passionate following, referred to in some cases as "cult-like"—which from a shareholder standpoint is certainly a good thing (think Harley Davidson).

Kris: Apple understands that their customers want quality and user-friendly products that work for their lives; and the fact that their products are also "cool" doesn't hurt their case. Whether the customer is a tech-savvy 25-year-old or a 65-year-old who wants to learn, they seem to be drawn to Apple products and—perhaps more importantly—to Apple Stores because they know Apple cares about them as users. Apple makes believers out of many of us, even before we own one of their products. We are hungry for what we've heard about the "Apple experience."

Chuck: I love the feeling you get when you walk into the store. It's clear to me that the company and its employees are there to make important things happen for their customers. They have a great "customer back" approach, and they're adept at using their technology to create incredibly satisfying customer experiences. They are all about *technology to serve the user, not users to serve technology*. Whether it's a family who wants to capture and creatively share their memories; a business person who needs mobile access to stay in touch with her team; a music-lover who wants to access to her entire album collection wherever she is; or a graphic designer who needs the most effective way to develop his projects, Apple maintains its focus on the outcome the customer needs. They remain relevant by tailoring the technology to the outcome that matters to the customer.

Joe: I don't know of any store of any kind that has more of a distinctly identifiable "vibe" than an Apple Store. The vibe, to me, is engagement. People are actively, even passionately, engaged with the products, the concepts, and each other's interests. The great lesson for any of us is to consider how to create that kind of engagement with our own customers.

Some claim that, because they are in a business so different from Apple, there's no way to transfer the lessons. But that's complete baloney. While it may indeed take some effort and creativity, there is just no reason that, regardless of what you make or sell, you can't create passion around it with your customers. It's simply a matter of distinguishing your organization's version of the Apple experience.

Kris: My 20-something daughter recently bought an Apple computer. I asked her why she chose Apple. She said, "There is less chance of getting a virus; it's fun, it's sleek, it makes me feel cool, and I can easily fit my whole life into it." When I asked her about her purchasing experience, she told me, "I made an appointment to buy. When I showed up, they met me at the door and introduced me to a sales person who never left my side until I had made my purchase. He asked me how I would use the computer for my work, my life, my entertainment. He made me feel as though there were no stupid questions. He listened and addressed the issues I asked about; in fact, he answered the questions I *should* have asked. Once I made my decision, he swiped my credit card right there. I realized that I had been educated, that I made a better purchase because of this sales person's guidance. I left the store a very happy customer." Wow.

Chuck: Apple's product education and support is focused on outcome—what is it you want to achieve, not a dissection of the technological aspects of the products. They have clearly looked at their products from an intuitive standpoint and are intent upon delivering as much empowerment as possible by anticipating how customers wish to use their products versus simply learning it from a detailed technical standpoint.

The first question out of the Apple associate's mouth from whom I bought my first machine was: "What is it you would like to do with your computer?" This differed greatly from a one-way dialogue I had in some of the big-box stores in which a sales person would tell me what I "needed." The levels of support are intensely customized for purchasers, depending on what they want the product to achieve. It's a reflection of the very conscious culture they've developed to support their vision of customer empowerment. I appreciate the "diagnose before prescribe" approach.

Kris: Apple's method of anticipating how a customer will use the product makes all the difference. When a salesperson talks to me about technology, I hear about 1 percent of what he has to say. But if that same sales person talks about how the product will *help* me, or be *fun* for me, I'll hear every word. Why would we consider buying from a company that does any less?

And, by the way, the whole concept of scheduling an appointment with a "genius" (their term for the technical experts in the store) is genius itself, in my book. I realize that the idea of scheduling an appointment can take some getting used to. However, once you realize that this works *for* instead of against you, you quickly become a convert. After all, would you still consider scheduling an appointment to meet with a genius an imposition if you knew that your questions would be answered, your problems solved, and you'd feel empowered? Probably not!

Chuck: I am always surprised at the demographic mix I encounter attending one of Apple's classes or witnessing in-store support. From high-school aged "geeks," to 30-something business people, to octogenarians—you see it all. And by listening to the conversations, you can literally hear the intense focus that's placed on outcomes and personal empowerment.

The store employees are trying their very hardest to help people produce what they truly want. I love the breadth of customer they serve; I think it highlights the fact that they're helping people do things that matter to them. And that is something that has no demographic limit.

Kris: The demographic mix is one of my favorite things to notice when I visit an Apple store. Where else do you see an 18-year-old sitting opposite a 65-year-old with both intently focused on a product and what it can do for them? On a recent trip to an Apple Store, I found myself so touched by the sight of a young Apple employee sitting nose to nose with a 60-something at a computer that I actually took a photo. I thought to myself, "Look at how engaged these two are with one another! She is mesmerized because he took the time to understand her needs and knows exactly how to help her. He'll show her the right product; and then he'll give her the best gift by empowering her with the knowledge she needs to use it." There was no question in my mind that this employee felt what he does matters.

Joe: I totally agree with Chuck and Kris's comments about the Apple experience. It's amazing to see how a store in a middle-American mall can bring together people who, by appearance, seem so different. I don't want to go overboard, after all. It's just a music player or a computer; and it's just a store. But, for anyone who is seeking an example of the power that comes from aligning people and strategy, it's positively inspiring.

Of course, I can't claim for a fact that *every* single Apple Store creates the kind of experiences that I've observed. But the consistency of experience in the four stores that I did visit (Nashville, Chicago, and two in Minneapolis) is impressive, to say the least. The same energy and enthusiasm on the part of both Apple customers and employees was present in all of them.

Chuck: Customer experience is another area that the brand really seems to emphasize. Nothing is left to chance; the in-store experience is centered on showcasing their products that are beautifully designed in a very open format. No stuffed shelves with tangled cords, poorly placed pricing labels, and confusing messaging.

Employees wear colored T-shirts that signal their level and type of expertise. In many stores, employees can also check customers out on hand-held devices to speed up the purchase process and help avoid lines. The backs of many stores contain crowded amphitheaters where Apple employees conduct free classes for customers on a range of products and, more importantly, the solutions those products can create. Employees wear devices in the stores I have visited that enable them to communicate across the store with one another. Whenever I've been referred to an associate in another part of the store, he or she greeted me by name and was already aware of my problem because the referring employee gave them this information.

Kris: Apple stores *do* have a vibe that you can't help but feel. It struck me that the younger employees all look exactly as they would anywhere else you might see them; in other words, no one has forced them through a corporate sieve. They all have colored T-shirts on and are beaming with confidence and passion. They truly seem to take pride in where they work and in knowing they are perfect for the job they are doing. They certainly know more than we do about their products, and they really seem to appreciate the opportunity to share their passion and knowledge. It's fun for them and beneficial to us; and it's both refreshing and contagious!

Chuck: When I was converting from a PC to a Mac, I asked one of the Apple employees how the start up would work. I wanted to be able to get rid of all of the promotional programs that normally clutter computer screens with offers and test programs. He said, "You just take it out of the box and plug it in. There is none of that to get rid of. We know it aggravates customers, so we don't think when you get your new Mac you should have to do that. We want your first experience to be a great one." My thought was: Are you kidding me?! Don't other computer makers also think it aggravates their customers?! Of course they do, but they choose a different experience that they believe serves them better.

Kris: This is the reason I want a Mac computer. I love it that the product is specifically designed to aggravate me less!

4

CUSTOMER EXPERIENCE—It *Is* YOUR BRAND

THE WAY THEY MADE YOU FEEL

Chuck: Have you ever recommended a place or person with whom you've done business to someone else—and found yourself going on and on about how great they were because of the way they made you feel when you interacted with them? You may talk about it in terms of the service they delivered, the fact that they recognized you even though they have hundreds (or thousands) of customers, or that they seem to actually anticipate what you want and have a knack for giving it to you without you even asking.

These are organizations that you feel operate the way *you* would if you were running them. And these aren't experiences that only happen once in a while; this is what it's like every single time you come in contact with them. Oh, there may be the occasional slip; but when it does occur, you find yourself making excuses for them in your mind: "They must be shorthanded today . . . or that must have been a new person at the counter. . . . That won't happen the next time I come in." You tell yourself these things because they have traditionally performed in a way that has earned them your forgiveness—so that, on the rare occasion that they *don't* live up to their incredible standards, you are willing to "give them a pass." These are the organizations that you believe "get it." In fact, if you didn't know any better, you'd think they could read your mind or had some type of "insider information" about you.

PRICELESS

This is true customer experience. This is what intentional design that's consistently executed by employees empowered to do so can look like. Have any doubts? Then just listen to yourself as you extol the virtues of your favorite restaurant, store, or brand of clothing as you recommend it to another person. This type of marketing is priceless. In today's wired and connected world, there is no campaign, billboard, website, direct mail program, or television or radio commercial in the world more powerful than your personal, passionate recommendation to a friend or colleague. People do not put their own credibility on the line with others—specifically, those who trust their judgment—unless they are certain that the brand or company will back it up. When a company causes you to advocate on their behalf, they understand that they must deliver quality products or service repeatedly, or they risk eliciting the exact opposite response.

Think back to a time when you have shared or heard a story about a bad experience. These types of discussions can bring out rarely demonstrated animation and passion in people as they describe their horror stories about the interactions they had with companies who were more than willing to take their money but completely under delivered on their experience. Fortunately, they will just as enthusiastically share animated, glowing reports about the wonderful encounters they've had with your company or brand.

Whether positive or negative, all of this takes place because an experience—intentionally designed or completely left to chance—intersects a key *moment of truth* with a customer.

INTENTIONALLY DESIGNED AND ARCHITECTED

The term *customer experience* is equivalent to the sum total of all interactions your customer has across all of your channels and venues that forms their impression of doing business with you. The good news is that this resource can deliver tremendous value when it is intentionally architected to expedite and enhance the delivery of your business strategy. The other side of the coin is that, left unattended, it can be your undoing.

Very few leaders want to go to bed at night knowing their customers' overall experience is an unplanned and uncoordinated collection of behaviors that leave the customer feeling disappointed at key touch points. The message to these customers is, "We're not certain we really want to take the time to learn about you and determine how to serve you in a more engaging way." The customer's reaction is then likely to be, "It appears you're not really much different than anyone else, so I'll look into cheaper alternatives." In today's world, do we really need to add a level of self-inflicted commoditization on top of our markets' already competitive nature?

WHAT IT'S LIKE TO DO BUSINESS WITH YOU

Joe: Customer experience is quite simply "what it's like to do business with you." I submit that it's the same definition that you can apply to brand—*your customer's perception* of what it's like to do business with you. The experience you create for them is your brand, and its strength is critical in achieving your vision. Therefore, every encounter that you have with your customers must be driven by—and in alignment with—this vision. There should be a clear reason behind every single aspect of every interaction you have with customers. Every point of contact creates a customer experience, and every customer experience either advances or hinders the achievement of your vision. So consider the following:

- How do you greet customers on the telephone? With a memorized "welcoming pitch" that runs together so fast that no one can understand it? "Good-morning-thank-you-for-calling-Acme-Balloon-and-Widget-Company-where-service-is-our-top-priority-this-is-Glenda-how-may-I-direct-your-call?" The telephone greeting to customers is your *brand*. Does that greeting help you to achieve your vision?

- How easy is your website to navigate? What is it designed to accomplish? Does your website make it easy to do business with you? The experience that your website delivers is your brand. Does the design of your website help you to achieve your vision?

- Does your advertising tell a story of what's true about your company, or a story about what you *wish* was true? If there is the slightest conflict between what you promise and what you deliver, then you create distrust in your customers. Until there is actual customer contact, your advertising is your brand. Does it help you to achieve your vision?

The point, of course, is that customer experiences either occur by chance or by design. Intentional leadership will bring people and strategy together by devising customer experiences that support and advance your vision. This will ensure that customer encounters are the result of planning, employee training, and culture—and the creation of processes that guarantee consistent delivery of the intended experience.

EXPERIENCE CREATES BRAND

Consider how customer interactions support and develop your brand. For example, one of my friends says to me, "Joe, I can meet you later this afternoon, but first I've got a meeting with my stockbroker." I ask, "How's that broker working out for you? What's she like? Are you happy with her and her company?" My friend's response expresses the brand of that broker and her company. Make no mistake about this, all of the advertisements about how this brokerage firm can make financial dreams come true are meaningless compared to my friend's answer.

Ten incredibly effective and successful leaders of 10 different companies can—and probably will—have 10 different *lenses* through which they view their businesses. One of the most effective of these is the "brand" lens (with *brand* being defined as your customer's perception of what it's like to do business with you). Viewing your business through this lens means asking the following questions with every decision you make, no matter how large or seemingly small:

- Does this *build* our brand?
- Does this *communicate* our brand?
- Does this *strengthen* our brand?
- Does this *damage* our brand?
- Does this *change* our brand?
- Does this *protect* our brand?

THE POWER OF ALIGNMENT

Creating a great customer experience is all about the incredible power of alignment. If your brand promise is that you are the most efficient, low-cost airline, then think about what you need to see when you are looking through this lens in order to bring all of your decisions into alignment. Consider:

- who you hire
- how you set up your route system
- what, if any, food you serve on flights
- whether or not you charge fees for extra baggage
- how quickly you "turn" planes between flights
- what kind of airplanes you buy (only 737s, or others as well?)

You may be thinking, "This sounds like Southwest Airlines"; and you're right. These are the kinds of decisions—all of which relate to the alignment of brand and customer experience—that Southwest Airlines and other great companies think about all day long.

YOU DO NOT OWN YOUR BRAND

A critical key to brand management is understanding that *you do not own your brand*. In fact, you don't even have possession of it. It instead resides in the minds of everyone who has an opinion of your company. I won't ask you if I want to know about your brand; indeed, you'll probably be the last person I'll ask. Rather, to discover what your brand truly is, I will ask your customers because—and we cannot emphasize this enough—*their* perception of doing business with you is your brand. Your advertising constitutes only your brand up to the point of any degree of customer experience, and this includes second- or even third-hand customer experience. Hearing someone say, "You know, I've heard that that company just looks for any way they can find to charge extra fees," tends to trump all the ads "that company" has ever run. Nothing is more powerful than customer experience in brand management.

THE EXPERIENCE ASSET

Chuck: The overarching reason to consciously leverage customer experience is because it is an asset that can drive results that accelerate your business strategy. While there is nobility in designing great customer experiences—and treating customers well in and of itself—it is its power to enhance and expedite the delivery of your strategy that make it so valuable. Quite simply, this is one of the most meaningful (and underleveraged) tools in our competitive arsenal.

The experience asset is similar to the others we have discussed in that we must design it intentionally and apply the same question: What is the best way to utilize this resource to accelerate the achievement our business strategy and vision?

It's critically important to remember that our efforts in customer experience are *value adding* versus *value consuming*. To spend time and energy engaging in activities whose return is unclear or nonexistent does not fulfill our obligation to stakeholders. That we can drive additional value *because* of how we serve customers—rather than *in spite of it*—is a foundational premise. We cannot confuse these.

As Joe mentioned, perhaps nothing supports our brand more than well-orchestrated and compelling encounters. What we sell, deliver, and provide wrapped in an innovative and purposeful experience is a powerful combination in any market. While products and services are getting easier to copy and reverse engineer, a well-designed experience—grounded in the best customer information available and executed in a purposefully designed culture—is almost impossible to replicate. It can become your "secret ingredient," your Coke formula, your Kentucky Fried Chicken recipe. Imitated? Possibly. Replicated? Never.

WHY NOT MORE FOCUS?

Certainly that brings up the obvious question, "If there is so much value here, then why don't more companies focus on this?" We believe that there are several reasons why a resource with so much potential impact is often left to chance:

- In many cases, no one in the company has taken clear ownership for developing an integrated and cohesive approach to the design, or execution of a coordinated customer experience across functional areas and channels. At best, there are isolated pockets of excellence (i.e., a great website or in-store encounter), which, while good in their own right, fail to account for the fact that customers don't isolate their experiences by channel or functional area. They want their overall company experience to be consistent at every touch point.

As an example, a bank client recently told me of their efforts around experience strategy and explained how they had constructed a "knockout" (their word) online banking experience that they felt would help them exceed their quarterly deposit goals. They truly did have a very impressive online experience.

However, after the quarter results came in, it seemed that total deposits had actually gone *down*. Their analysis showed that, in fact, deposits had gone up for the customers that were the highest users of the online experience. The message from that segment was, "We like it; let's see some more." However, there was an offsetting message from the older, more established (and affluent) segment (who were less likely to partake in online banking): "I want to come into your lobby to do business face to face. Your lobby is continually understaffed, impersonal, and slow. I am tired of it and will take my large deposits elsewhere."

Moral: One experience cannot be spread across all customers and channels—even if one group loves it. You must have the right experiences for the right groups of customers. Had the bank's online segment been more profitable than the "in-lobby preferring" segment, the bank could have at least known there would be a trade off, and they might have chosen to create a more effective lobby experience in parallel with the online experience for those that preferred a more personal touch.

- Leadership in many organizations is simply too far removed from the actual delivery of their experience to clearly understand what is necessary to develop a thoughtful and effective design. We've also found that a fair amount of companies do not have any way to audit their current experience at an organization-wide level so that they can diagnose gaps and focus strategy on filling them.

The fact is that the majority of leaders are too distant from their customers' experiences to be able to understand this. Sure, they may receive an occasional letter about an issue a customer wanted to raise to a higher level. However, the reaction here is usually a response with the appropriate form letter—the one that assures the customer this was an exception and states that "we will work to make certain it doesn't happen again, and thank you for bringing this exception to our attention." But most leaders cannot, with any degree of confidence, tell you what *type* of experience is consistently delivered across their organizations at each of their customer touch points. The inability (or unwillingness) to see the aggregate view of the negative experiences drives a lack of urgency to act. What's not seen as a problem is not acted on. It's not that there is no problem; it's that there is *no awareness*.

- Some organizations know there is work to do, and are willing to do it, but they lack the process to get them there. Important work is seldom achieved without a guiding methodology or protocol. The good news is that, for teams seeking to use experience design as a tool to deliver maximum value, there is a clear process to do so.

There is an orientation in some circles of leadership that anything dealing with feelings or other intangibles can't really affect hard business outcomes. Tell that to customers who make decisions every minute as to whether or not they will do business with you based precisely on how they *feel* as a result of interacting with your organization and its brand. Do we discount the *feeling* of class, excellence, and status that Mercedes customers associate with that brand and experience? Or the experience delivered by the Ritz Carlton that makes customers *feel* special, welcomed, and "treated like ladies and gentlemen"? Or the *feeling* of wonder, excitement, and awe generated by a Cirque du Soleil show? Do we really believe these don't enhance value? It is much easier to see this in other organizations because *you are having* the experience, not trying to create it. And when it is done well, there is a level of effortlessness about it that is misleading in its simplicity and ubiquity. I've heard leaders say, "Well sure that works for Ritz Carlton, but we're not the Ritz." Well, the Ritz wasn't the Ritz until they decided to be.

CONSISTENCY OF PERFORMANCE

Joe: If you think about the examples of great customer experience that Chuck just cited—Mercedes, Ritz Carlton, and Cirque du Soleil—there's a common thread that runs through all of them: consistency of performance.

This is the great brand builder, whereas inconsistency of performance is the great brand killer. All of us can think of companies we do business with that, if there were truth in their advertising, would have to post a big sign outside the front door saying, "Feel lucky? Come on in. Depends on who you get."

We live in a society that celebrates the "superstar." Any business leader loves to get a letter or email extolling the virtues of a glowing performance by one of his or her employees: "I just wanted to tell you that Heather at your Fifth Avenue store went above and beyond the call of duty in solving my problem the other day." That's a great note to receive; and we should certainly recognize and celebrate that kind of performance.

However, what's even better—much, *much* better—is the note that says, "I just wanted to let you know that whenever I am in any of your stores, no matter who I deal with, I always receive great service." That's the ultimate testimonial; and that's when you know that the customer experience you create is building your brand.

One question I often ask when I'm working with company leaders is, "Think of the people on your team. Get their faces in your mind. Assume that I'm a new customer who asks, 'Which of those employees should I go to for a great customer experience?'" The correct answer, of course, would be, "Any of them." That's a difficult standard to achieve, but it's one to which we must all aspire. The cliché about not being stronger than your weakest link has never been truer than when applied to the customer experience.

So how do you achieve the kind of consistency of great customer experience that builds a brand into a powerhouse? You achieve it with:

- vision
- culture
- strategy
- relevance
- employee engagement
- process
- communication

In short, designing and delivering a great customer experience is intertwined with every other facet of your business. As Chuck pointed out, customer experience cannot be separated from everything else. It's part of the fabric of the entire organization that is woven through everything that you do. There is not a single job in your organization that does not ultimately impact your ability to provide great customer encounters. Even those employees that are far removed from direct customer contact have a "ripple effect" impact on the experience you deliver because of their effect on other employees.

WHO MANAGES THE BRAND?

A few years ago, I was the keynote speaker for the annual SPECS event. SPECS stands for Store Planning, Equipment, Construction Services Seminars and has been exclusively produced by Chain Store Age magazine since 1965. My audience was top retail store planning, construction, maintenance, and engineering executives.

I opened with this question, "In your company, who is responsible for brand management?" The most popular answers by far were the marketing, advertising, or sales department.

I knew that there was a group of store planning and construction executives in the audience from a national grocery chain with which I was familiar. I identified them and asked them to share their opinion about the width of the aisles in their stores. I knew that this store had particularly wide aisles and so was not surprised when they said that this design made the shopping experience easier and more pleasant for their customers. I told them, "That customer experience is your brand. Therefore, you are responsible for brand management. In fact, because there isn't a job that exists anywhere in any company that doesn't ultimately affect customer experience, *every employee* is responsible for brand management."

As a part owner of a restaurant, I am constantly attuned to the hundreds of things that affect our brand all day long each and every day. I went one evening with my wife to have dinner, and after sitting at the table for a few minutes, I felt that something wasn't quite right. I finally realized that there was the tiniest bit of static coming through the sound system playing background music, like when you're listening to the radio and the signal isn't coming in quite clearly enough.

At that moment, our brand—due to the "auditory experience" we were creating for our customers—was static. I immediately went to Stephanie—our amazing bartender and a master of creating fabulous customer experiences (and award winning martinis!)—and asked her to check on the music. Within a few seconds she had corrected the problem. The brand was back on track.

I'll never forget my experience at a resort hotel where I was speaking to a business convention. Early one morning, I walked through the lobby of this mostly family oriented hotel and was absolutely jarred by the blast of music emerging from their sound system. At 6:30 AM, they were playing Guns N' Roses' "Welcome to the Jungle." Now, being an old rocker myself—and Guns N' Roses fan—I've been known to rock out to "Welcome to the Jungle" myself on more than one occasion. But that song—playing in *that* hotel lobby at *that* hour—was completely and totally destroying the brand. The customer experience was more like what you'd expect (and want) in the lobby of a Hard Rock Hotel.

I remember being utterly flabbergasted that no employee— and especially that no manager—seemed bothered in the least by this obvious incongruence. However, it was no more surprising than what we've all seen when we witness a manager walking through a store of intolerably long lines of impatient customers. He or she often seems absolutely oblivious to the fact that there are unhappy buyers and that the brand is being destroyed by a less than acceptable customer experience. The manager obviously has more important things to attend to.

The point is that, whether it's the width of the aisles in the store, the quality and volume of the music, or a long line of customers, it's all customer experience. And all customer experience is brand.

THE POWER OF A SMALL EXPERIENCE

Chuck: Several years ago, we took our first family trip to Disney World. Everything about the trip was what a parent would want it to be for their children's first vacation to the Magic Kingdom. As we all know, there are Disney stories galore about the great experiences in the parks, restaurants, and hotels. But one of the greatest memories I have came from a small, seemingly insignificant experience that I doubt even the person delivering it remembers. I still tell it to this day, though, because it is such a great indication of the power of intentionality applied to experience design and embedded in the everyday operations of a business.

On our second day there, my youngest daughter and I hopped into the small car to tour the "It's a Small World" exhibit. She was sporting her newly purchased Goofy hat, complete with the big droopy ears. When our excursion ended, we got out of the car and exited the exhibit. About five steps down the walk, I noticed my daughter crying. Seems she had lost her Goofy hat. We returned to the ride, and I approached the Disney employee attending it and explained the situation.

The young man said he would look through every car as it came around to find it for her. He returned in five minutes with disappointing news: He could not find the hat. I saw tears well up in my daughter's eyes so big that, had they hit the ground, they would have made an audible sound.

The young employee pulled out a piece of paper. "What's your name, sweetheart?" he asked. "Andrea," she said, choking back tears. He wrote for a few seconds and then handed her the paper. "Andrea, do you see the Disney store down the street? I have a friend there named Monica. You give this note to her, and she'll take care of you." I pulled him aside to let him know that I didn't have the receipt and couldn't really prove when and where we had bought it. "No worries," he whispered. "Just enjoy the rest of your time here."

Andrea couldn't wait to get to the store. I'd be less than truthful if I told you I didn't have a bit of skepticism about what might happen. Not wanting to have her feelings hurt a second time, I was trying to manage her expectations and express that, while I'm certain the nice young man had meant well, sometimes these things don't always work out as we hope they will.

"But Dad, he said don't worry."

We found Monica and my daughter handed her the note. "Andrea, I've been waiting for you. Craig called me and told me what happened. We can't have you at Disney World without your Goofy hat! You go through the store and find any hat you like." When Andrea found the one she wanted, we returned to Monica. I was waiting for the, "Oh, I see you chose the more expensive one. We'll just do some paperwork and your dad can pay the difference and you can be on your way" response.

But no such response came. Instead, Monica offered, "Let me cut the tags off for you and, if you like, here's a pen and you can write your name in it just in case. I'm so happy you found a new one, and I hope you have a great time the rest of your vacation."

No earth-shattering pronouncements; no grandstanding. Just a simple gesture that was exactly the right one, delivered without hesitation, at exactly the right time for exactly the right little customer.

Now, did Disney's stock rocket that day as a result of those small gestures? Of course not. But it did in our household. And don't think for a moment it was an accidental event, because *nothing* at Disney lacks intention. The clarity of their intent; the processes used to empower and engage their employees from the customer's viewpoint (the only one that really matters); and their ability to execute on a moment's notice using their discretion are magnificent.

And, by the way, I don't think I've ever seen two young people so personally pleased to cause such a great outcome on behalf of one of their young customers as Monica and Craig were. Employees will always be engaged and proud to work for an organization that trusts them to do the right thing when it needs to be done without jumping through hoops. Well-designed customer experiences are as engaging for our employees as they are for our customers.

What is the argument to *ever* leave this to chance?

THE MAGIC FORMULA

As with so many things that appear effortless, well-crafted customer encounters seem to simply happen by magic. However, there is no magic formula here; there is simply focused and purposeful work conducted by dedicated leaders whose goal is to drive value for their customers, employees, and shareholders. Not as sexy as magic, but certainly more meaningful.

We have discussed some of the companies that do a fantastic job of delivering a distinctive customer experience, which in turn creates measurable value for their organizations. While each is totally different than the other, they have several foundational similarities in their customer experience strategy that any organization would benefit from. In working with clients, we find the following approaches to be the most effective across a wide variety of industries and companies:

- First and foremost, "make the decision to go"; in other words, *fully commit* to using customer experience to accelerate your business strategy. Make it clear throughout the organization that this will be a hallmark of your value proposition;

- Next, create an end-state view as to what your experience should look and feel like at *every* single customer touch point. A first-rate experience in one area only to be followed by a haphazard one in another should be considered a failure. Beginning with the end in mind, "empathically engineer" your way back from there. Put yourselves in your customers' shoes, and develop an atmosphere that will cause the customers to feel brilliant about their choice to do business with you. Leave absolutely nothing to chance in advancing this outcome on your customers' behalf at every turn. Guide this quantitatively with research and qualitatively with input from your employees—especially those on the customer-facing side of the business (sales, service, call centers, billing, etc.). This is where some of the best information comes from; and if you want to see engaged employees, simply inform them that they will be chosen to design how their company will "show up" in front of your customers. You'll be amazed.

- Once their experience vision is in place, choose a partner with a proven methodology for the design process. To stay on track with your goals, assign accountability for the plan's delivery and have it report directly to the top executive team.

- Make absolutely certain the experience is simple enough to execute consistently and effectively across all channels (this should be part of the design methodology). While a great deal of thought goes into design, its execution has to be highly predictable and operationally efficient. This means minimizing over engineering the experience in order to empower employees to make immediate decisions to support it instead of having to interrupt it to "talk to a manager" (a bad experience in and of itself).

- Define the experience well beyond the transaction at hand; look for the touch point where it first begins and carry it through until the last opportunity you have to positively impact your customer. In many cases, this never ends because of the relationship's ongoing nature. For instance, one of the banks we work with has defined the beginning of their customer experience to be the moment a customer thinks about changing banks. All of their point of sale material, online presence, call centers, advertising campaigns, and lobby teams are designed with this in mind. They truly believe you get one chance to make a good first impression—and they never waste it. They also believe their experience never ends, which is emphasized by their dedication to even stay in touch with customers *who have left them* because they moved, found another bank, and so on. The result? They have the best customer recapture success rates of any of their competitors.

A FUNDAMENTAL BUILDING BLOCK

While magic can certainly be fun to watch, we all know that it is misleading and involves a great deal of illusion. To achieve our vision and strategy, our customer experience delivery must be straightforward and authentic (which certainly doesn't rule out fun!). Companies that deliver the greatest contribution to their strategic progress by using an engaging customer experience realize that this is not a transactional or temporary commitment. It is one of the fundamental building blocks of your brand. Those who lead the way in experience design and management recognize this. They intentionally plan and seek input from customers and front-line employees in order to maintain the highest level of execution and relevance. They know that, once started, there is no finish—simply a continuous stream of intake, assessment, and constant improvement. Additionally, they are aware that, by taking this approach, what also never ends is the ongoing value driven by this well-executed commitment.

Five questions to ask yourself about Customer Experience:

1. Are the customer experiences that you create intentionally designed to answer the question, "What type of experience do we need to deliver to our customers to accomplish our vision?"

2. Is the experience consistently executed across every touch point you have with your customers? Do you have an inclusive "touch point management strategy"?

3. Do you know how your experience is significantly different from those your competition delivers?

4. On a scale of 1 to 10, how easy are you to do business with?

5. Does top leadership own and regularly audit the customer experience in your company? How close are they to the front-line experience you deliver?

Case Study

PINNACLE
FINANCIAL
PARTNERS

Joe: There's an idea shared by many successful companies that states that, of all stakeholders in a business, employees should come first. The thinking is that, unless employees are engaged, satisfied, and care deeply about their work, there's no way to fulfill other stakeholders' needs.

A company that I have referenced in some of my other books is a remarkable bank in Tennessee called Pinnacle Financial Partners. I am a Pinnacle customer myself, and I have done business with them as a consultant. For my money, there is no better example of intentional leadership or the alignment of people with strategy.

From its inception, Pinnacle has developed a dual vision to be the best financial services firm *and* the best place to work in Tennessee. A very strong case can be made for the first assertion; but I want to focus on their second goal here. The philosophy shared by Pinnacle's management—and so effectively executed by the intentional leadership of president and

CEO Terry Turner—is that the key to getting and keeping clients is having employees who are knowledgeable about and committed to delivering exceptional service. They believe that well-informed and satisfied associates result in well-cared-for and loyal clients. They also feel that they couldn't achieve their vision of being the best financial services firm if they didn't create a workplace that attracted and retained the best financial services professionals.

So how are they doing? Who says that Pinnacle is the best place to work in Tennessee? Well, *Business TN* magazine has said so for two years in a row; and the *Nashville Business Journal* has agreed that this is the case for six consecutive years.

What, you might wonder, has Pinnacle done to become the "best place to work"? It's something that any company can— and indeed *should*—do. Terry Turner believes that three critical practices—recruitment, retention, and engagement—must all be priorities and work together. From a Pinnacle e-letter that Terry Turner sent to clients and employees, here are a few of their practices.

RECRUITMENT

- Get the right people in the right jobs. Continually recruit for new talent, just as you recruit new business.
- Focus on candidates with deep experience and successful track records in your industry to avoid mismatches.
- Avoid hiring people who are discontent in their current jobs. Instead, look for people who are happy and successful. The candidates most likely to succeed are those who have been successful in the past and enjoy doing the work.

RETENTION

- "Wow" every associate from the first day by blowing them away with your passion for meeting their needs. It can be costly, but invest the time to thoroughly orient them to your brand and how they fit in.
- Set company-wide retention targets. Pinnacle has a goal of 95 percent against which managers are evaluated.
- Build a strong sense of family and encourage close personal relationships. Employees might quit impersonal employers where there is no emotional engagement, but they won't leave genuine friends and family.

ENGAGEMENT

- Excite your associates and motivate them to deliver exceptional quality. Reward team performance to remove competitiveness and encourage cooperation across the company. Good companies have great individual performers, but the whole team has to work together to get to the next level.
- Measure employee satisfaction by conducting regular work environment surveys, and hold managers accountable for their teams' results. Insist that managers continually communicate using a variety of channels and tools.
- Emphasize where the company is winning more than where it is losing. People work best out of their strengths, not their weaknesses. Fuel their successes.

With Pinnacle, as with so many extraordinary companies, we see once again that there's nothing particularly exotic or complicated going on; there's merely focus and consistency.

The intentional leadership at Pinnacle made being the "best place to work" so important that it became part of their DNA. They talk about it all the time. They measure their progress and reward excellent performance. They hold leaders accountable for making the "best place to work" part of the vision and becoming a reality.

At so many companies, there's an abundance of slogans and a shortage of execution. At Pinnacle, they succeed at their vision because it's not a slogan; it's how they do business all day long, every day.

Special Report

Events As Strategy

"The problem with communication . . . is the *illusion* that it has been accomplished."

—George Bernard Shaw

AN ASSET, RATHER THAN A COST

Joe: Almost every company has meetings and events for employees. Some companies also have events that bring customers or vendors together. We have seen the significant positive effects of properly designed and well-executed company meetings and witnessed ways in which companies have begun significant transformations from the catalyst of a great event. Unfortunately, we have also seen the incredible waste of time and money that results from events that lack purpose and focus. We feel so strongly about the potential power of corporate meetings and events that we have included this Special Report: Events As Strategy.

We hope that this report changes your thinking about company events and allows you to see them as an asset, rather than a cost. Most importantly, we hope that, from this point on, you *never have an event that doesn't advance your strategy*.

THE IMPACT BARELY SHOWED UP

Chuck: I remember a debriefing session we held following what we thought was one of our more productive business meetings. We were undergoing the introduction of a new business strategy and had decided that, since all the right leaders would be in attendance, we would use our regular annual business meeting to deliver this important new information.

We analyzed the post-meeting survey and read comments about the meeting's value, what the attendees took away, and what they considered key messages to be. About halfway through the review, the SVP of marketing from my team looked at me and said, "Did they go to the same meeting we did?" Rather than the hoped-for comments about how we had helped them understand and advance our strategy, the majority of the commentary focused on the food, entertainment, and the golf outing (not to mention the comments about the weather). The impact we had wanted to make—and had worked on for months—barely showed up in the feedback.

We failed to accomplish the intended result for that meeting. We had so many things in motion that weren't aligned with our strategy that we now faced an unsavory choice: to hold another event in order to emphasize the new strategy and cultural changes we had designed to meet our business challenges or accept a less than desired return on the most important work we had done in years. Neither was acceptable nor a good use of our shareholders' money or our employees' time. We had taken what should have been one of the most important events in the company's history and significantly decreased the return on our investment. To say we were demoralized would be an understatement.

A MEASURABLE RETURN

Our executive leadership team vowed to learn the hard lessons from this experience. We realized that the responsibilities for the meetings' outcome were ours alone. We knew we got the poor feedback because of the event we had designed—simple as that. It was therefore our obligation to execute these events in a more meaningful way; and so we set about making certain we would never repeat these mistakes.

We committed to developing a competency around the delivery of events that would create measurable return. We established a relationship with a leading event production company that clearly understood where we wanted to go and had the expertise to deliver on that (since we had clearly proven we didn't). We were relentless in our introspection as we sought to improve at this. We recognized that we had to be completely aligned with the delivery of our vision and strategy—and that the potential power of a resource like this could never be left to chance.

TOO MUCH VALUE LEFT ON THE TABLE

Kris: Who hasn't taken a break from the office to board a plane headed to a company conference (hopefully some-place warm!)? Many of us with corporate jobs have had this experience.

Of course, going to a meeting or an event doesn't always mean getting on an airplane. Wherever the meeting or event is held, however, there are some questions that naturally come up. What does it mean? Why do we do it? Is it a valuable use of time? Will there be networking opportunities? Will I get to know leadership, employees, or customers better? Will the event be engaging? Will it affect my thinking? Will it be worthwhile?

You may indeed feel that *all* of the corporate meetings or events you have attended were valuable experiences designed with a clear outcome in mind. I suspect, however, that many—or even most—of the professional events you attended were those in which any specific, strategic outcomes were pretty much left to chance. In many cases, "it's that time of year" or "because we always do" seem to be the only reasons behind these often expensive, usually time-consuming conferences.

Countless companies leave far too much value on the table because they hold their events for the sake of holding the event—as opposed to doing so *only* when there is a strategic purpose for it. This is an unfortunate truth, especially in recent times, when the purpose of meetings has been under intense scrutiny. Some companies cancel meetings as one of their first cost-cutting measures during economically challenging times. But doing this also eliminates an absolutely vital means of engaging their employees or customers in the interest of advancing strategy. We firmly believe that the intentional use of company and client events is one way to accelerate business strategy that's not only smart—it's necessary.

I have worked on all sides of the meeting industry over the better part of the last two decades, and I have seen many companies merely follow trends instead of lead with purpose. Why are so many corporations willing to spend big money on their events without a clear outcome in mind? They'll write fat checks for the motivational or celebrity speakers and the big-name entertainment, which certainly isn't wrong *if* it helps create a truly effective event. But rarely are dollars spent that are tied to a clear purpose. Why spend the money unless you know precisely why you're spending it?

ADVANCING BUSINESS STRATEGY

Kris: Leadership should determine the need for an event with the purpose of advancing business strategy. When approached this way, the planning team can design the event with a clear focus on the specific, measurable result they want to create.

Bear in mind that this is no subtle shift. It's a snap-your-head-around change from holding an event because "It's our annual meeting. We do it every year," to "We use our event to advance our business strategy." What a difference!

Designing successful, impactful meetings is not easy work. It takes clear vision, purpose, objectives, and the right partners to get the job done. In addition to the executives responsible for the meeting, there are often many other players involved. Meeting planners (internal or external), a travel company, a production company, a speaker's bureau, possibly an agency, a hotel, presenters, and employees are often all on the team. Without a clear appreciation for the vision, strategy, and intended outcome, these parties are disconnected—and often have very dissimilar ideas about what a successful event looks like.

EVENT FOR EVENT'S SAKE WAS OVER

Chuck: It was not unusual at all in our previous approach to begin our event-planning sessions with a statement like, "Well, it's time for our annual sales meeting (or leadership meeting, employee meeting, etc.); let's talk about what we should do." While scheduling events with some predictable frequency is certainly required to plan well and do things like secure venues, we wanted to alter the mindset completely. Our focus shifted to what communication, learning, team building, and other qualities were needed to catalyze the progress of our vision. We found this approach to be much more effective because it constantly made our goals the focal points for all behavior and activity. Without that context, it was easy to wander off into the weeds and distract ourselves from the reason we were holding the event in the first place. And given the nature of our business and market at the time, we knew we could not waste any resources we had available to us.

Too many of our previous planning sessions focused on filling time slots to make certain we didn't have any downtime. The prevailing thought was that, if you are going to get everyone together, you want to make certain they are busy doing *something*—even if that something wasn't even remotely tied to our strategy. We realized as we got better at this that if we were searching too intensely for content maybe the timing wasn't right for the meeting and we would reserve the right to postpone or cancel it until it served a more deliberate purpose. Our fundamental shift was from *event because it's time*, to *event because our strategy requires it*. This drove us to align our events with our strategic planning cycle; and because strategy doesn't change simply because the calendar does, we did not want to have meetings simply because it was a new year.

When everything you do is intentionally designed to answer the question, "How does this help us move closer to our vision?" an interesting thing happens: All activity becomes grounded in an outcome and a clear context for why you are doing it in the first place. Perhaps more than anything, we found this shift in orientation to create highest return on the use of our resources.

SIMPLICITY AND ACCOUNTABILITY

What we wanted to get from our meetings and events would be grounded in how it could drive progress in our strategy. We boiled down our approach to some simple guidelines: How will the event be designed to accelerate our strategic progress and what are the evidence points that we succeeded? If we couldn't be specific on our answers here, then maybe there was no need for a meeting. We were unforgiving in this regard because we knew the outcome started and ended with us as leaders and that all great outcomes are directly related to the quality of the input and design.

DESIGN CONTENT THAT COULD BE
STRATEGICALLY REPURPOSED

To increase the return on our investment—and add significant continuity to our ongoing communication strategy—we improved our skills in developing event content. Specifically, we created a clear strategy to leverage this content in our *post-event* communication with multiple stakeholders across multiple venues. Once we had an event planned, we had a fixed cost element—regardless of what the content was. We decided we could add more value to our effort by going into the event knowing exactly how we could, with small incremental cost, establish, document, and edit the content for use in our overall communication strategy. We simply began by asking ourselves, "How could we devise our content so that we could intentionally capture and edit it to support our ongoing communication strategy with clients, employee teams, analysts, and so on?"

One of the most effective things we did took place during a combination client and sales event designed to launch the significant repositioning of a 90-year-old company brand. We interviewed clients as they entered the event, and again the following day as they left, to compare their "before and after" perspectives of our strategic direction. The feedback was incredibly positive, and we were able to repurpose the video feedback for use in employee meetings. It served to bring them closer to our clients and build their confidence in our new direction. We even helped local plant managers present this material in a way that more strategically positioned them in the eyes of their direct employee teams.

We used other content edits in a presentation to our board of directors to demonstrate our accountability for the capital we had requested to develop this new strategy and brand work. We then used it in our contract bid presentations with potential clients to let them see how we were perceived by their industry peers.

The bottom line: The movement of *events for events sake* to *events as strategy* adds a significant high-value asset to a leader's portfolio of tools for accomplishing their business strategy as effectively as possible.

WHAT'S THE POINT?

Kris: I have had the opportunity to contribute to extremely successful events in which everyone on the planning team has clearly comprehended the vision and intended outcome. All partners (executives, meeting planners, the production company, outside speakers) were included in strategy and communication planning discussions from the beginning. Everyone on the team could answer the question, "What's the point?" When working with a focused team like this, creative ideas flow and are on target, and conversations don't go in circles. Every idea is clearly focused on one specific goal. Every decision is aligned to a specific outcome. Planned messages are clear, and every part of the event is aligned to these messages. All elements—such as executive presentations, videos, outside speakers, set designs, presentation graphics, the look of the room, even entertainment options—are meant to create an experience that will deliver the company's intended result. Working as part of a team like this and producing a truly successful event is incredibly satisfying and fulfilling work.

A GAME-CHANGING APPROACH

Chuck: We had the opportunity to apply these best practices when I was leading a company that provided products and services to the financial services industry and their customers. We were experiencing a time in our history where our core business was coming under significant pressure from changes in technology that were making it less relevant to our clients and their customers. Our charter was to develop a new growth and brand repositioning strategy that would create new competitive advantage and allow our clients to see us as a more relevant partner. As we completed the new strategy, we wanted to get into the market quickly and effectively in order to take advantage of what we believed would be a game-changing approach in our industry. The tool we chose was a series of well-orchestrated events to open this next phase of our company's history.

A CRYSTAL-CLEAR VISION OF OUTCOMES

Our first step was to develop a crystal-clear vision of the outcomes we desired and then use these to implement the event's design and execution. Specifically, we wanted:

- Clients to understand our new strategy quickly, see our new solutions as more relevant to their most critical business issues, and, as a result, view us as a more strategic partner;
- To reposition our sales people in our clients' eyes and grant them better access to top client decision makers—because of the solutions and knowledge they represented;
- Measurable, quantifiable results; it was important to know if we could make the events themselves self-funding;
- To capture content from the events so we could edit and reuse it in our overall communication strategy for internal and external stakeholders. This would create the most return from the events' fixed costs, while adding consistency and efficiency to all of our ongoing communication.

The next step was to design the content *completely* from the client perspective. We started with the most intractable issues our clients were facing (which we learned through our research). We then introduced well-known thought leaders in these specific areas to share their perspectives with our clients as to how they could more successfully tackle these problems. We made certain that the speakers were well versed in the client issues so the content was not only relevant, it was highly customized and usable.

We positioned this event differently from any others we had done. Instead of being a selling event or product launch, it was a strategic contribution we wanted to make as a partner "on behalf of our clients" to help them be more effective in their own strategies. It was all about them and their strategies—not us. This was a major shift in our client event thinking, which historically had been events focused on talking exclusively about our products and services. We were certain if we executed this new format properly and made it our primary focus, our company would accrue countless benefits as a result.

Our next step was to leverage these events more efficiently than we'd done in the past. We invited multiple stakeholders in order to more quickly convey the message about our strategic change and brand repositioning, gain critical mass, and let them experience it more personally. Our final roster included our sales teams, chosen supply chain partners, board members, and key officers from our executive leadership team—as well selected line employees from across the company who we had invited as a reward for their good performance.

Finally, we made certain the execution was flawless at the event itself. We held our new solutions presentation until almost three-quarters of the event had been completed to stay true to our commitment to make the event about our clients and *their* most pressing problems. It was critical in order to accomplish our goals for us to demonstrate our commitment to move from "here is what we make and sell" to "we will leverage our resources on your behalf to solve your most pressing issues." It was especially important to impress upon our clients the cornerstone of our new brand positioning: "We are better off together than apart; we win when you win."

WE SURPASSED EVERY OBJECTIVE

So how did we do? We were able to return to our board of directors and say we had surpassed every objective we had established:

- Regarding measurable results: Our rate of contract renewals and retention for the clients at the event improved so much versus our norm that *this alone* more than funded our expenses for every event we staged. Client enrollment in our new solutions occurred more quickly than any service we had released before (61 percent of the clients signed up *on the spot while at the event*); and revenue objectives were delivered well ahead of plan.

- In the pre- and post-event research we did to validate the new image we wanted to develop, 98 percent of our attending clients told us they saw us as a much more strategic and relevant partner, planned to extend their contracts with us, and would recommend us to other nonclients in our industry. They raved about the opportunity we gave them to network with one another and rally around important issues they had in common.

- Our sales teams expressed (through surveys) that they felt this was the most engaging event of which they had ever been a part. They claimed that they could now elevate their relationship to a higher level in their clients' organizations. Client decision makers validated this as well, saying we had earned a "seat at the strategic table" given the new focus and direction we were taking. Fully half of those in attendance volunteered to help codevelop and beta test new solutions with us.

- Client interviews, along with videos and executive thought leader presentations, were captured and edited in order to provide tools for all levels of leadership to use as we took our new vision and message to 8,000 employees. This became the foundation for our internal change management strategy and allowed all of our employees to gain a perspective as to how their "new" company's clients saw them. This was in fact the most powerful tool in all of our change management and strategic repositioning work.

- We also edited content to be used in Wall Street presentations to analysts, at our board meetings, and for recruiting/new employee orientations. This was a message we wanted all stakeholders to receive.

In our strategic debriefing, we identified several key approaches that led to the success of this new event strategy:

- Starting with a clear outcome and vision for the events.
- Establishing hard metrics to validate and quantify the return.
- Leveraging the fixed event costs by having a plan to capture and repurpose content so we could use it throughout our organization.
- Focusing on specific client issues and staging our solutions in that context; thinking "client back versus internal out."
- Not using any "filler content"; every moment was purposeful and driven by our vision and outcome.

- Choosing an excellent event management production partner and including them in our strategic planning early so they could develop a strong, focused execution plan.

While we pushed hard to quantify our results to the greatest extent possible, the best evidence of our success was anecdotal—and came when we reviewed our results at the next board meeting. One particular board member had been especially skeptical, challenging our proposal and request for funding when I had originally presented our new strategy. He did not think it was the time, given the recent challenges, to be funding what he referred to as a "client party." After reviewing the results, he sat quietly for a moment, letting all of the other board members give us their input. He then raised his hand and asked us why we weren't planning to do five more of these as soon as possible!

Kris: In the case study above, outside professional speakers and business experts contributed significantly in making the event a success. We didn't think about them as content fillers. Although their content was excellent, the thing that mattered most to us was that they understood that we were casting them in strategic roles in order to orchestrate the best possible experience for the attendees. There was no room for ego or canned speeches.

Companies today are looking for relevant event speakers who give interactive and authentic presentations with valuable and actionable ideas. They are interested in an off-the-shelf presentation. In other words, the decision maker wants to see up front that real value is tied to the presentation.

Outside experts and speakers are often woefully underutilized. You can greatly increase your speakers' effectiveness and value if you include them in the event's planning sessions. You must make sure they know exactly what the purpose of the meeting is and how the event will be designed to accomplish the objectives. Any outside experts that you use as speakers need to know that they won't be a disconnected keynote dropped into the middle of a general session; they will fit like a piece of a solved puzzle. In most cases, speakers who are given this kind of information will have great ideas about how they can be most effective. Think about it: Who has seen more meetings that work (and those that don't) than a consultant or expert who has spoken at hundreds of them?

As you broaden your thinking about what the speaker can offer, consider also what you believe to be the nature of a "speech." The traditional "talking head speech" is one-way communication at best, whereas conversational, interactive presentations are often much more effective in accomplishing your objectives. A dialogue that takes place on stage can be incredibly engaging for the audience. Employees love to see their executives get out from behind the lectern and just talk with them like a "normal person." An on-stage interview with the leader of an organization (by a skilled interviewer) gives employees a chance to see their leadership's true energy and passion.

A SPEECH THAT ISN'T SPEECHY

I recently worked with a young speaker who is an expert on Generation Y. When you see him present, all you can think is, "Thank you. A speech that isn't speechy!" He is constantly reacting to the audience by inviting participation, challenges, and questions throughout his entire appearance. It's the anti-speech—and it's highly effective. Why? He is authentic, he knows his stuff, and he is willing to relate his presentation to each organization.

Corporate events audiences are getting younger all the time, and they tend to respond to interaction and conversation much more enthusiastically than they do to a speech. An executive—even a well-spoken one—behind a podium giving a one-hour speech with Powerpoint (particularly if he is *reading* the Powerpoint) will rarely be able to fully engage a 23-year-old employee. All you have to do is look around the room in this kind of meeting and notice the younger people checking out. A speech like that is so unbearably boring to them that I think they (and, to be fair, probably plenty of the veterans, as well) often use the time as an opportunity to catch up on emails and Twitter updates.

Think about how this younger generation gets information. They get what they need instantly. They don't respond to or trust anything that seems "slick" or "canned," and they expect material to be current and relevant. If it's not, they move on immediately. Why would anyone ever think that a young employee would sit still and listen to *any* presentation that isn't interesting and engaging for a full hour? And the same holds true for any employee of any age. Bottom line: If the presentation is boring, it is quite literally a waste of everyone's time.

THE SERIOUS SIDE OF FLUFF

Kris: Let's talk about what is often referred to as the "fluff" element. I'm using "fluff" to refer to the fun or entertaining part of an event. The fact is that the "fluff" can serve a very serious purpose. Sometimes entertainment is the perfect way to surprise the audience, disrupt their thinking, and get them to engage.

Getting people out of their left-brain thinking and into the right brain increases the chances that they'll think more creatively.

Something that seems like "merely" entertainment at first glance can actually be a vehicle for increased effectiveness. What some might call "fluff" may be the very catalyst for inter-action, engagement, and the kind of thinking that can help a company advance its strategy.

Think about entertainment the same way you do speakers, and consider what you want to achieve. Call a corporate entertain-ment buyer or agent who is experienced in working with corpo-rate meetings and events. Tell them about your event, audience, and budget, and be clear with them about the experience you are trying to achieve. This aspect of your event can and *should* be an integral element in helping you accomplish your objectives.

A CATALYST

We hope that this Special Report acts as a catalyst to create some new thinking and serious conversations about the "why" and the "how" of your meetings and events. We think that events are, for most companies, a hidden asset that they rarely take full advantage of. The fact is there is no form of com-munication—no e-zine, no newsletter, no email, no poster, no video—that can realize the power of a shared vision more effectively than physically bringing your people together.

So don't waste this asset. Design and execute your corporate meetings and events with fully intentional leadership. Know *exactly* what you want to accomplish and how you are going to advance your strategy with the opportunity of your next event. And if you're having a meeting just because "it's that time again"—don't. Save everybody's time and money and wait until you are focused and purposeful. Invest the time to plan and design an event that will make a significant difference in your business.

Top Ten Meeting Mistakes

1. Having a meeting just because you "always have a meeting."
2. Going into the meeting without stated objectives and a clearly defined outcome.
3. Putting more focus on what the executives want to say than what the audience needs to hear.
4. Overloading the schedule without giving participants time to network, process, and just catch their breath.
5. Focusing on only one mode of communicating (i.e., a podium parade of talking heads), as opposed to looking at multiple ways to communicate with and engage the audience.
6. Poor coordination and communication between/among speakers, resulting in conflicting messages or unnecessary repetition.
7. Making no provision for building on the meeting's objectives and goals after the event.
8. Structuring the event so that the audience is completely passive, not allowing them to interact and affect the meeting and its content.
9. Not updating the meeting's structure to reflect changes in the company, the audience, or the culture at large.
10. Not utilizing a production company that understands how to help you design and produce an effective, strategic event and make the most of your investment.

5

THE INTENTIONAL LEADERSHIP MINDSET

DEFINED BY ACTION

Chuck: When we refer to intentional leaders, we mean those who are grounded in a similar philosophy that enables them to more effectively embody the concepts we have cited throughout *Never By Chance*. It goes well beyond style; these leaders have a portfolio of traits that are grounded in a belief system that makes their actions almost second nature.

First and foremost is the conviction that leadership is not defined by the position itself, but by the action and behavior demonstrated while *in* the position. These are people who love the *work* more than the job or the title. They see the position as a beginning opportunity from which they can do great things—not an end in itself ripe with special benefits and treatment. They clearly comprehend that they will be judged not by having attained the position but by what they accomplished while in the position and the manner in which they did it. And they go about their work accordingly.

The second important orientation is that these people view leadership as an obligation, not an entitlement. Given today's high-profile media coverage of some incredibly bad leadership behavior, it must seem oxymoronic to many to use the words "leadership" and "obligation" in the same sentence. Fortunately, these reports, although they make great headlines and ratings, do not represent the vast majority of leaders who are focused on doing the right things on behalf of their customers, investors, and employees every day.

In stark contrast to higher profile cases, these leaders understand that there are responsibilities that they alone are uniquely positioned to fulfill and deliver and that by doing so they can catalyze an organization to greatness. They also realize that, given the magnitude and complexity of these responsibilities, if they choose to ignore or leave them to chance, the organization's value will suffer.

A client CEO I worked with emphasized this point to me when he said, "One of my most important obligations as the leader is to create a compelling vision for my company and then create a culture to achieve that vision. I have over 10,000 employees in my organization. If I am not doing my job—fulfilling my obligation to establish a clear and articulate vision and strategy for our future—how likely is it that this large group of employees will one day say about me, 'You know John really doesn't seem to have this whole vision and culture thing figured out. Next Thursday morning, the 10,000 of us are going to get on a conference call so we can build a vision and culture for this company'? Not very likely." Leaders such as John know the responsibilities they must meet and obligations they must fulfill to drive their companies to their full potential. Intentional leaders are fanatical about starting with an end in mind that is grounded in how to deliver sustainable value for every customer, employee, and shareholder. Why? Because they know that there will be tough times as well as good times and that clearly focusing on an aspirational view of success can bridge people across the chasm in challenging times. Working from the end state back will ensure that their road leads to the right destination. These leaders see the outcome as theirs to define, communicate, and support in order to realize its potential. When asked, "Why are we doing what we are doing?" there is not a moment's hesitation in their response because, to them, there's never a question. They have worked with their teams to calculate precisely how every single resource will be deployed toward this end and can articulate it on demand.

CLARITY

Joe: In the almost 30 years that I've been working with leaders of companies of all kinds, shapes, and sizes, I would have to say that the concept of *clarity* stands out as one of the most critically important leadership factors. Almost without fail, when an organization finds itself in trouble or struggling, it's the result of a lack of clarity. That's why so many meetings take place with people sitting around the room, nodding in agreement about what needs to be done—which then never is. There was either a lack of clarity around the vision, mission, or strategy; about who was truly leading; or about who was accountable.

One of the strengths of great leaders is that they are understood; everyone knows where they stand and what they stand for. People may not *agree* with the direction they're taking, but there's no confusion about what that direction is. From military leaders like the Civil War's controversial yet incredibly effective Gen. Ulysses S. Grant, or Winston Churchill in World War II, a great leader is, if nothing else, clearly understood.

President John F. Kennedy demonstrated this kind of clarity of leadership in a speech to a special joint session of Congress on May 25, 1961, when he said "I believe that this nation should commit itself to achieving the goal, before this decade is out, of landing a man on the moon and returning him safely to earth. No single space project in this period will be more impressive to mankind, or more important for the long-range exploration of space; and none will be so difficult or expensive to accomplish."

President Kennedy laid out the vision clearly and very specifically and then gave the reason for the vision. Finally, and perhaps the most powerful element in his entire statement, he said, "none will be so difficult or expensive to accomplish." He made a clear declaration, a stake in the ground, a line in the sand. To say that this is what we're going to do, here's why, and it's going to be hard as hell, that's what gets people behind a vision. Not just clarity, but in-your-face honesty as well.

INCREDIBLY OTHER-CENTERED

Chuck: One of the most notable characteristics of intentional leaders is their other-centered, "on behalf" orientation—their perspective that they do what they do for customers, employees, shareholders and not for themselves. They are dedicated to helping their stakeholders and only benefit personally when they do so in a sustained and effective manner. Inflated ego and selfishness have no validity here. Valuable leaders fulfill their sense of self solely by creating success for their teams, fulfilling the obligation of leadership, and remaining aware of the fact that they've set their organization up for maximum achievement. For those who understand the concept of obligation, it could be no other way. These are leaders who love the *work*, not the trappings of the position.

In his best-selling work *Good to Great,* author Jim Collins noted this "other-centeredness" when he referenced what he called "a compelling modesty" that he noticed in the extensive research he conducted on leaders' impact on long-term results. Those great leaders did not aspire to be put on pedestals; they simply wanted to quietly go about their work, credit others, and produce extraordinary results. Why? They were driven by their love of the work, ability to focus on an outcome, knowledge of their role in catalyzing it, and working closely with their teams to deliver it *on behalf of others*—not themselves.

These types of leaders understand that, when they lead, others must follow. They know that, when they take their companies into the marketplace battle and look over their shoulders, there will actually be people following them! Not because these people have been coerced or are afraid, but because they clearly comprehend where they are going, why, and how what they do every hour of every day matters in reaching their destination. The crystal clarity of the "end in mind" approach draws them to follow because they can see and feel it for themselves and because their leadership's intentional engagement of everyone at that level led to this understanding. This is competitive advantage to the *nth* degree. Can you say that about your organization?

MAKE IT PERSONAL

Joe: It's been said that extraordinary companies are made up of ordinary people who care deeply about what they are doing. Too often, people in management positions merely assume that everyone in the company cares as much about what they're doing as the leaders do. Yet in order for employees to care about the company's vision, the company must become as relevant to employees' lives as it is to customers'. Just because the revenue numbers turn the CEO on doesn't mean that those numbers are going to do the same for front-line employees.

At the most basic level, intentional leaders are very good at answering this question for all stakeholders: What's in it for me? Why should I support your new quality program or your customer service initiative? Do I even know why you, as our leader, are passionate about it? If not, why in the world should *I* even begin to be passionate about it? You don't have to give me a "rah rah" motivational speech; just show me that you care. Because, until I know that you care, I won't even begin to.

I interviewed a top-performing hotel manager and asked him what he felt the key was to gaining employee engagement. He said that, for his employees to be interested in the life of the company, he had to demonstrate that he was interested in *their* lives. For him, that meant everything from showing that he understood the challenges that the housekeeping staff came up against on a daily basis, to knowing that the desk clerk's daughter was competing in a softball tournament on the weekend.

If you have thousands of employees, the challenge of showing that you care becomes daunting; but you have to meet it, nonetheless. Whether you do it through town hall meetings, company site visits, or even regular video or email communication, every employee should personally feel their leader's presence. After all, how can you lead if you're just a name to them? You have to make it personal—because it is.

THEY KNOW THEMSELVES

Chuck: Leading with passion, conviction, and sustainable energy requires you to do the difficult work of knowing yourself from the inside out. Leading with intention necessitates a very high level of comfort with change, especially since much of that change will be directed at the leaders themselves. They are in a constant state of self-assessment and continuous improvement to better serve their organizations.

There are many tools and resources for leaders who understand the need to be familiar with their own strengths and weaknesses. But, for those who choose to deny or simply remain in their protected comfort zone, little exists. In order for this trait to be successful, desire must precede insight and effectiveness. Such leaders therefore attain a level of conscious competence that lets them utilize their skills on demand and as needed for any situation they face. They know that along with the hard work of developing self-awareness comes the reward of authentic leadership—an "in the zone" style where work can provide regeneration rather then the degeneration often found in leading from a contrived style or approach.

These leaders clearly recognize the notion put forth by author Stephen Covey in *The 7 Habits of Highly Effective People*: that, in nature, only the human species has the opportunity to manage the moment between *stimulus* and *response* and to consciously choose how to respond to a stimulus, versus reacting intuitively as an animal might. They learn and apply how to manage this gap in a manner that creates confidence, passion, and focus for themselves and their peers. They know their behavior is a product of choice rather than conditions that are out of their control. For this reason, they proactively, thoughtfully, and purposefully deliver what they must achieve on a consistent basis instead of reacting to every stimulus that comes along, causing a chaotic atmosphere that can stress an organization unnecessarily. They remain "on their game" in even the most trying times. In this way, they are not only more effective, but models for others in their organizations as well.

These self-aware leaders—focused on outcomes and leveraging all resources to that end—are not worried about their weaknesses being "discovered." They know that no one possesses *every* skill, so they concentrate on minimizing these weaknesses and focusing on their strengths. They do not waste time or energy trying to create an aura of perfection because they know this is more about the leader's personal ego predicament than the outcome he or she is tasked to deliver. By knowing themselves—both their assets and their limitations—they make better hiring decisions because they know how to resist the urge to hire in their own likeness. It is precisely this awareness that allows them to find complementary resources that support and accelerate their company's progress toward their vision.

These managers have a clear sense of their area of impact. They know that they are always "on" and that every moment in front of those they lead is an opportunity to communicate their message, model the culture, and passionately convey the vision they have so purposefully designed. For this reason, they get up every morning with an "impact plan"—a conscious approach to the messages they will deliver and how they will convey them to everyone they encounter during the day. They know precisely how they will show up each day, and they never waste an opportunity to engage a stakeholder. They live with an "if not me, then who?" attitude that screams personal accountability.

This leader also believes that hesitating means regressing and is a passionate advocate of personal continuous learning and improvement. You cannot stand still in a forward-moving environment and expect to do anything but fall further behind, whether from a personal or an organizational effectiveness standpoint. That is why their zest for nonstop knowledge is surpassed only by their desire to act on it. They have an insatiable curiosity to learn more, be more, and cause better outcomes on behalf of customers and employees by virtue of this education.

Perhaps more than anything, these leaders understand why people follow them. This recognition is not arrogance, but rather self-awareness that's tied to their belief that they are obligated to understand this in order to be as effective as possible. With this in mind, they know they will always lead with intention and purpose, remaining aware of what works and why it works. This authenticity is their personal leadership vision, which, when achieved, has the intended consequence of infecting their entire organization.

CONTINUOUSLY IMPROVING

Joe: A great leader maintains a healthy balance between relying on the foundation of rock solid values that rarely (if ever) change and the constant change necessary to stay competitive.

The motivation to learn is driven by their awareness of what success means: that you know what *used* to work. You may be a master at competing and winning in markets that no longer exist; but what about today, to say nothing of tomorrow?

Every leader in every company I have ever assisted agrees with this statement: In order to stay competitive, we have to be better tomorrow than we were today. In 30 years of consulting I have never had anyone say, "Actually, Joe, we really don't have to improve. We're just fine the way we are, and we don't anticipate improving anything for a few years." Of course not. Every leader agrees with the idea of continuous, even relentless improvement.

I have a follow-up question to the statement about being better tomorrow than you were today. I ask, "What did you do yesterday that made you better than you were the day before?" This is where I usually begin to lose eye contact with people. While everyone—certainly every leader—gives enthusiastic lip service to the idea of continuous, daily improvement, it's rare that anyone can cite *exactly* what they did to improve.

A continuously improving and learning organization is led by a leader who does the same. Nowhere, except possibly in the area of ethical behavior, is the principle of leading by example more important than in the area of consistent education and growth. An effective leader can't send a message that says: "I want all of you to learn. As for me, I pretty much know it all." The fact is that the most important lessons of all are the ones we learn *after* we "know it all." We can't become caught in the "expert trap." In truth, we are all pretty ignorant at the beginning of our careers—not unintelligent, but ignorant. We simply don't know how things work. Over the years, we learn, we get smarter about how things work, and we begin to develop confidence. Sometimes that confidence grows into believing that we have become experts to the extent that we now in fact know how *everything* works. But remember what success means—that, in fact, what we know is how things *used* to work.

If you're smart—and surely if you're a leader who never stops learning—you work your way out of expert and back up to ignorant. You wake up every morning wanting to know how things work *today*. One expression of this idea that I particularly liked was the aspiration to "go to work stupid every day."

Too often, ideas like "continuous improvement" and "learning organization" become empty slogans, almost obligatory phrases that a leader feels that he must use. On the contrary, improvement and learning are the most active and ambitious of undertakings that require daily attention and perseverance.

INCREDIBLE SIMPLIFIERS

Chuck: Mark Twain is given credit for the quote, "If I had more time, I would have written a shorter letter." Twain knew how difficult it is to create a message that is succinct, purposeful, and understandable at a personal level. We suspect he also knew that taking the time to do so made the impact of his message exponentially greater.

Today's markets and business situations are anything but simple. Complex competitive issues, integrated partnerships, disruptive technology, regulatory environments, and so forth require a substantial amount of brainpower to understand and formulate strategy—let alone communicate the essence of that to tens, hundreds, or thousands of employees to understand at a personal level.

It was once said that great leaders are also great simplifiers who cut through argument, debate, and doubt to offer information that everybody can understand. This is not lost on intentional leaders who "empathically engineer" their messages, who are able to put themselves in their followers' shoes and express the message so that it means the most to each person receiving it. I was once asked if that means "dumbing down the message," the answer to which is an emphatic *no*. It has nothing to do with intelligence and everything to do with appreciating that every person has experiences and perspectives that influence how they learn and internalize new information. An intentional leader knows that his or her goal is to effectively convey the essence of their vision and strategy in a way that every individual "gets it" and understands their role in making their company successful. A self-serving, ego-feeding, "I'm obviously smarter than all of you" approach to communicating has no place in an intentionally led organization.

One of the things that we have noticed about how these leaders engage their teams is that they have developed a promise or covenant with the organization to always *deal in reality*. They fully recognize that no employee should ever feel as though they received anything less than true forthrightness from their leaders. However, they also remember that their job is to inspire hope and possibility whenever they can. For that reason, tough messages are always connected with their perspective on *why and how* they will succeed in spite of the challenges ahead. Not an airy, high-level, "everything will be all right" false assurance, but a well-developed, fact-based response delivered with confidence and certainty that makes clear the reason their company will manage through hard times and prosper.

Whether you lead tens, hundreds, or thousands, the opportunity to lead is one of the greatest rewards in a career. To do so with intention, purposefully guiding and aligning an organization to create its greatest success, is a true privilege.

Five questions to ask yourself about Intentional Leadership:

1. How would the members of your organization answer the question, "Why are we doing what we are doing?"
2. What is your personal development curriculum for self-improvement and continuous learning as a leader?
3. Does the leadership in your organization *deal in reality* when communicating with employees, openly discussing issues and how the organization will successfully overcome them? Are employees given the opportunity to engage and interact in these discussions?
4. Do you take time to purposefully plan how you "show up" every day in front of those you lead? What is your process for regular feedback on how you are doing from those you lead?
5. Are you more enamored with your *job* than your *work*?

INDEX